NAPA VALLEY PICNIC

A California Wine Country
Travel Companion

To our elders and ancestors, the generations who have worked this land with digging stick, fire, pick, hoe and plow. It is to them that credit is due for the richness of any given day spent savoring the

Napa Valley.

JB

To Miss Koster, who taught us the value and beauty of language and art.

KS

Napa Valley Picnic

A California Wine Country
Travel Companion

by
Jack Burton & Ken Stanton

BORED FEET PRESS

Mendocino, California

www.boredfeet.com

© 2002 by Jack Burton and Ken Stanton
First Edition, October 2002
Printed in the United States of America on recycled paper.

Book design by Elizabeth Petersen
Cover design and book composition by
*   Wendy Blakeway-Clayton of DesignXperts*
Cover basket design and maps by Marsha Mello
Front cover photo by Kaarin Svendsen
Back cover cartoon by Elizabeth Leeds
Edited by Donna Bettencourt & Bob Lorentzen

Published and Distributed by
Bored Feet Press
Post Office Box 1832
Mendocino, CA 95460
(707)964-6629, (888)336-6199
E-mail: boredfeet@mcn.com
Web: www.boredfeet.com

Library of Congress Cataloging-in-Publication Data
(Complete data available from publisher).

Burton, Jack, 1951-
        Napa Valley picnic : a California Wine Country travel companion : great picnic spots, favorite wineries, picnic sources, menus & recipes, stories & diversions/ Jack Burton and Ken Stanton -- 1st ed.
        p. cm.
        Includes bibliographical references and index.
        ISBN 0-939431-26-2
        1. Picnicking. 2. Menus. 3. Napa County (Calif.)--Guidebooks. I. Title.

10 9 8 7 6 5 4 3 2 1

Contents

Preface

Napa Valley Picnic is the second work in a series of conversational and amusing California Wine Country travel companions. It is written by series creator Jack Burton, a Sonoma County chef with a penchant for picnics, and Ken Stanton, a Napa Valley winegrower/author intimate with his celebrated neighborhood. Together we'll introduce you to the people and history of Napa County, California, as well as guide you to the numerous enchanting picnic places.

Napa Valley Picnic serves as a handy and practical guide to a world-class wine region only an hour's drive from the San Francisco Bay Area. With our focus on picnicking, we'll guide you to the culinary artisans, farms, ranches, and wineries that make Napa County an epicurean paradise.

An underlying theme to our book is the enduring and beautiful native stone bridges of Napa County. Between sixty and one hundred of these masterpieces were built across the Napa River and its tributaries. In the 1850s local pioneers built wooden bridges, but these lasted only fifteen years on average, and replacement costs became prohibitive. Achilles F. Grigsby, member of a notable pioneer family, was the first to advocate stone bridges.

According to surviving records, the Valley's first stone bridge was built in Napa in 1860, crossing the Napa River at First Street. Though steel later became available, stone was the material of choice for its low cost. Local volcanic stone, usually rhyolite, was quarried on Howell Mountain, Mount George, and near Calistoga. Expert stonecutters, working for $2.50 to $3.00 per day, could build these enduring monuments in a few weeks. First a wooden 'falsework' was framed, then the bridge was built outward from the footings to the center. A horse-operated hoist put the stones in place.

Once a bridge opened, being roughly eighteen feet wide, common courtesy dictated that one horse-drawn vehicle wait for the other to pass. Notable artisans included H.W. Wing, J.B. Newman and R.H. Pithie, the latter responsible for both the Pope Street and Putah Creek bridges. The Putah Creek bridge, now submerged beneath Lake Berryessa, was known as the 'Queen of Stone Bridges,' at nearly 300 feet the longest stone bridge west of the Rockies. Drive slowly through Napa County and look for these amazing structures built in the horse-and-buggy era yet still safely accommodating the heavy flow of modern vehicle traffic.

So without further ado, won't you join us in the circle from earth and grape to picnic table and glass?

Welcome!
Jack Burton and Ken Stanton

1

Welcome to the Napa Valley Neighborhood

St. Helena Sunday Morning

I had gone out early to wander up Spring Street on the edge of the predawn darkness. It's shift-changing time for all the critters who make their livings in the small wilderness that borders White Sulphur Creek. A wisp of fog crept low among the alders like a silent incantation to the esteemed rising sun.

The frogs were now sleeping off the evening's festivities. They had started their jolly work around midnight with their singing for love, and they kept at it until the first blush of morning.

An old raven was rattling his prayer beads in a mossy oak tree, and a passel of crows were getting the spirit, high in a cathedral of stately firs on the far hillside. A covey of quail were down in the creek bed taking the holy water of ancient sacred thermal springs that mingle steaming with cool mountain runoff.

I saw a fox cross the road, plus much more evidence of comings and goings down by the waterside. One of the joys of the Napa Valley is encountering so much nature only a short stroll up into the hills from busy Highway 29.

I had been out taking in the pleasure of daybreak. When I returned to the cozy Hotel St. Helena, I found my wife snug, back under the covers, with two steaming mugs of coffee by the bedside.

"What's going on out in Napa County this morning?" she asked.

"The raccoons have been fishing about down in the creek," I said, and sipped my coffee, "and the skunks and 'possums have shuffled off to bed."

9

"The night herons are full of lusty frogs and have gone back to their roosts," I added, "and the woodpeckers are just waking up with acorns and the juicy larvae of wasps on their minds."

"What about the crows?" she inquired.

"The crows are still in church up on the hill, but they're gonna be plenty hungry when they come down to town," I replied.

"Me too," said my wife. "Let's walk up to the Model Bakery and plan a picnic!"

This book tells how to plan you own Napa Valley picnic and picnic menu and where to find your picnic supplies at our wonderful local food shops and outlets.We suggest convenient recipes and places to picnic all over Napa County's gorgeous countryside. The book also serves as a practical tour guide to wineries, restaurants and other diversions you might enjoy in the area. The book organizes the Napa Valley neighborhood into four general areas: South Valley, Mid-Valley, North Valley, and the Eastern Hills and Valleys.

White Sulphur Creek near St. Helena

Whatever your mode of transportation, a day's sojourn will reward you with the opportunity to enjoy vineyards, lakeshores, riverfront, redwood forests, friendly small towns or gorgeous parks. Wherever you actually stay in the Napa Valley will make a fine focal point and starting place for your trips and adventures. Everything you need for the day's picnic is readily available within a short, pleasant drive or walk.

Napa Valley Overview and History

The Napa River Valley has long been home to people enjoying the bounty of a place exceptionally blessed by Mother Nature. Only 180 years ago, this land of vineyards and wineries was overflowing with the abundance of the natural world and inhabited by a people who have been here longer than civilization, longer even than agrarian culture as we know it. It was a land where the water was pure to drink, herds of elk and deer grazed by the hundreds in the tall grass, and dozens of grizzly bear could be sighted in a single day. As pioneer Elizabeth Cyrus Wright has written, it lay "fresh from the hand of God, like a great unfenced park." The hillsides "wore their full dress of trees down to the floor of the valley" with "noble oaks scattered across the valley lands, no cut down trees, no stumps, save those trees that had died honorably of old age."

Perhaps Wright was a tad romantic. Renowned anthropologist A. L. Kroeber declares the Anglo notion of "an entire wilderness continent discovered" a fallacy. Native Americans, like the local Wappo people, managed the land for thousands of years using techniques like burning, tilling, transplanting desirable species of plants, weeding and irrigation, thus improving their ability to forage and hunt. The park-like forests clear of underbrush were products of careful management by the Indians. The Poet of the Sierras, Joaquin Miller, wrote that when the Indians of Mount Shasta were wiped out, the forests he enjoyed riding through on horseback with ease became choked with underbrush in thirty short years.

The Wappo, their name Anglicized from the Spanish *guapo*—meaning brave, for their resistance to foreign invaders—are considered to be among the oldest of California's native tribes, and occupied roughly the northern, central and southern Napa Valley. They hunted and traveled throughout the rugged mountains, but lived in the foothills or valleys. The Wappos consisted of three main tribelets, each occupying a cross-section of land containing mountain, valley and stream. They were the Mishewal, the Mutistul and the Meyahk'ama. Mount St. Helena, known to them as *Kana'moto* or 'human mountain,' was the spiritual center for all Wappo. Wappo legend tells of the people being created on the very summit, a place that became so sacred that none dared stand there.

A peaceful and uncomplicated people, the Wappo lived lives fully integrated with their spiritual beliefs. Private property was considered an immoral concept, as was forcing someone to do something against one's will. War was uncommon and for the most part ceremonial, usually ending as soon as one warrior died or was injured. Their basketry, along with the neighboring Pomo's, is considered the finest in the world. Revered elder Laura Fish Somersal, who died in 1990, made baskets of unmatched beauty and intricacy from willow and redbud. The weave could be made tight enough to hold water, and gift baskets might be as small as one inch in diameter. Somersal's basketry is displayed at the Warm Springs Dam Visitor Center near Geyserville in Sonoma County.

The Wappo traveled each year to the coast to trade for clamshells and to harvest, eat and dry seafood. Obsidian was one of the most important commodities for the Wappo, with the larger pieces too important to use in trade. One of the main sources of obsidian in California was at Glass Mountain, two miles north of St. Helena. The Indians used digging tools and in the process created large pits to dig out the best specimens. After blade blanks were created, these were taken to sites along the Napa River for finishing into spears, knives and arrowheads. California Indians made the largest flaked obsidian blades in the world, up to three feet long. Glass Mountain was reported by anthropologist R. F. Heizer to be literally covered by at least 100,000 cubic feet of obsidian flakes.

*black obsidian
arrow point*

Without the invasion of Europeans into this region by the 1830s, the Wappo way of life-in-balance may have continued indefinitely. However, over a twenty-five year period, disease, war, slavery and prostitution devastated an entire culture. Of the 4,000 to 8,000 Wappo living here in 1800, only a few hundred remained by 1900. In 1922 the last great Wappo leader Kanetuchma died at age 129. The people mourned for three days during which time they undertook "The Great Burning" where all vestiges of the past were destroyed because the people had given up hope. To make matters worse, in 1958 Congress passed Public Law 671, known as the Termination Act, in which the Wappo Tribe was effectively stricken from the federal record. Ancient tribal lands were confiscated and sold.

Then in the 1970s, the tribe reorganized, becoming a political force. In 1987 Senator Daniel Inouye reopened investigations of the Termination Act. Around this time the native plant garden at Bothe-Napa Valley State Park was created as a sacred place for Wappo to come and collect plants for basketry and other uses. Today efforts continue to gain federal recognition that could bring funds for housing, education, and purchase of lands that are available to other recognized tribes around the country. There is hope now for the future, for the children to learn from their elders the language, customs, songs, dance and basketry that are so much a part of this ancient culture from which we all may learn.

A Nutshell History of Wine in the Napa Valley

Napa's modern destiny as a renowned wine region largely resulted from a collision of its geological and climatic characteristics with the great surge of human migration during the California Gold Rush of 1849. Napa County lies within the folding and grinding zones associated with the San Andreas Fault system. Soils brought down from the surrounding mountains are the product of relatively recent geological activity and perfectly match the needs of the many vineyards the area is now famous for.

The history of the wine industry in Napa has followed a rocky road, with boom-bust cycles coming almost as regularly as the crops. The number and variety of disasters should warn us that, even now as we ride the coattails of the most spectacular boom in California wine history, the good times certainly will not last.

After settling in the Napa Valley, in 1838 transplanted Missouri mountain man George Yount was the first to plant grapes in the Valley, first near his homestead on Yount Mill Road, and later at the end of State Lane and in Rector Canyon. The growing Temperance Movement had convinced him of the evils of alcohol consumption, so those first grapes were for eating only.

By the 1850s, however, California was becoming well known for grape growing partly through the efforts of Agoston Harazathy in Sonoma. An obscure historical figure named John Patchett planted Napa's first commercial vineyard in the 1850s, but his name is usually forgotten in favor of Charles Krug, who founded Napa's oldest surviving winery in 1861. Krug did more for the development and promotion of wine in Napa than any other figure in the nineteenth century. He was Napa's ambassador of wine, similar to Robert

Mondavi's position today. For three decades after the Gold Rush, however, grapes were just another crop competing with the very successful wheat, tree fruit and cattle industries, and to a lesser extent, quicksilver. After 1868 and up until 1900, most labor in the vineyards was performed by Chinese, who were simultaneously discriminated against and tolerated because no one else could do the job so well.

Stone barn in Knights Valley

The 1880s saw a wine boom that would not be duplicated for nearly 100 years. It was precipitated by the unfortunate phylloxera root louse epidemic in Europe that decimated their industry. With the dreadful possibility of French wines becoming unavailable, Napa vineyard acreage, pegged at 3,500 in 1880, grew to a phenomenal 12,000 acres only two years later. California wine, especially on the east coast, had previously been snubbed by wine snobs as inferior to French, but when easterners began drinking California wine, they were pleasantly surprised. By the end of the decade, Napa wines took the Paris World's Fair wine competition by storm, in essence declaring to the world that Napa wines were the equal of French wines.

In the midst of victory lay the seed of disaster, hints throughout the decade being ignored or hidden by Napa growers. First an overabundance of wine in stock slowed new vineyard planting, and then the Panic of 1893 closed banks around the nation. Finally by 1900 the phylloxera scourge had pretty much wiped out the industry in Napa Valley, although a few isolated geographic areas like Foss Valley were curiously unaffected by the root louse.

Fortunately, alternative industries surfaced to prop up Napa's economy. The quicksilver mining boom was in full flower over in Pope Valley, and a bona fide gold and silver mine near Calistoga, the Palisades, brought in over a million dollars in its heyday. Olive trees replaced vines, and tourism grew mainly because of the hot springs resorts and the popularity of bottled mineral water, a product born at Napa's Soda Springs Resort.

In 1900 a chemist from Bordeaux, France named Georges de Latour became the key figure in rebuilding the wine industry not just in Napa but in all of California. Though George Schoenwald at Spottswood had first used the resistant rootstock named Rupestris St. George with great success, it was de Latour who imported millions of the bench-grafted vines for other growers. In the first twenty years of the new century, many new wineries were built, including de Latour's Beaulieu Vineyards in Rutherford, whose cabernets made by winemakers Joe Ponti and André Tchelistcheff were and still are legendary.

Just as the industry was poised for an unprecedented run of success, disaster fell with the passage of Prohibition in 1919. Loopholes in the Volstead Act allowed winemakers to continue their trade despite the law of the land. Oddly enough, many Napa growers made large profits in the next half decade by selling bulk wine to the eastern market where people could legally produce 200 gallons of wine for home consumption. Georges de Latour did very well throughout Prohibition by capturing the church sacramental wine market. By the mid-twenties, however, an oversupply of grapes and the passage of the Wright Act, which tightened the loop holes in Prohibition, began to have an effect. Prune orchards soon replaced the grapes.

The consumption of alcoholic drinks in the 1920s increased exponentially, and by the early 1930s, Prohibition was a national joke. Though many thought Prohibition would never last, it took longer to be repealed than expected, and it wasn't until 1933 that the Twenty-First Amendment was passed.

Now winemakers had the Great Depression to contend with. Winemakers like Louis Martini tried to jumpstart the industry, but for the next three decades prunes and other fruits would be as much a part of the landscape as grapes. Still, Beaulieu swept the wine competition at the 1939 San Francisco World's Fair, and made the best red wine in Napa for decades. Just a few large wine houses would dominate the wine industry during this period: Beringer, Christian Brothers, Beaulieu, Inglenook and Martini.

World War II initially took young men away from the labor force, but in a strange twist the war actually contributed to the Napa Valley wine boom when the French wine supply was stricken. Despite unprecedented national prosperity in the 1950s, wine grapes were one of the least profitable fruits to grow in California, returning on the average only $200 per acre. These were lean years for grape growers and vintners, without the romance of winemaking prevalent today. Then the wine industry discovered that holding wine-tastings across the country opened people's minds to their product, and by the mid-sixties, a wine boom was apparent to all. Robert Mondavi split from Charles Krug and built his own winery down in Oakville, only the third to be built since Prohibition.

In 1968 Napans, looking to the future, took advantage of a new state law to vote in a controversial agricultural preserve, allowing the trickle of newcomers to the industry in the sixties to become a flood in the seventies. President Nixon drank Jack and Jamie Davies' Schramsberg champagne at the White House in 1972. New wineries were popping up by the dozens. Then in 1976 came the momentous Paris tasting that put Napa on the world map. French judges in the now-famous blind tasting chose Chateau Montelena's Chardonnay and Stag's Leap Cabernet over France's best. Napa Valley has never been the same since that tasting. In the early seventies it was still possible to drive the length of the Valley after dark and not see a single car. Now everyone knew of Napa or wanted a part of it. By the end of the 1970s, sixty new wineries were established, and weekend traffic jams in St. Helena became regular events.

The Napa wine industry came of age in the 1980s, when big corporate money changed the face of farming here. Many wineries sold to foreign investors. The small independent grape growers—

Old carriage wagon, Pope Valley

once controlling perhaps 50 percent of grape acreage—began selling out to wineries who wanted more estate-grown grapes. One major indicator of changing times was the folding of the Napa Valley Co-op in mid-decade. It had been a mainstay for the small grower for fifty years. The pace of change in vineyard practices accelerated dramatically. Many experiments in trellising and canopy management, like leaf thinning and fruit thinning, became standard practice. Cutting-edge vineyard management and the highest quality wine went hand-in-hand, and those growers and vintners unwilling or unable to keep up were left behind.

In retrospect, the changes in the eighties and nineties were mind-boggling. Wine region appellations were established, a winery definition ordinance was passed to limit spurious commercial activities in an agricultural zone, a hillside erosion control ordinance was passed, and the art of pairing food and wine became an industry with the opening of the Culinary Institute of America at Greystone. In all these areas Napa led the way.

One hundred years after the last phylloxera epidemic, the bugs returned in a different form to decimate the industry again. Most of the damage occurred on the widely planted rootstock AXR1. Though the incredible St. George proved resistant, most growers did not return to this standby. A revolution in the grape nursery business came up with new or modified resistant rootstocks more appropriate for fine wine, like 110R, 5C, Schwarzmann and Boerner. Most growers had replanted by the mid-nineties only to be greeted by a new epidemic, Pierce Disease, spread by the blue green sharpshooter. Formerly a curiosity that dropped a vine or two in the summer, it was now killing hundreds of vines close to riparian areas.

As we embark on the new millennium, Napa Valley holds its own as the most famous wine region in North America, with five million visitors a year. It's an international destination with arguably more fine restaurants per capita than Paris, the venerable symbol of haute cuisine. One has to search closely for any prune or walnut orchards now, but one could argue that the grape monoculture that stretches from Carneros to Calistoga is a recipe for disaster. A new vector of Pierce Disease, the glassy wing sharpshooter, has destroyed the wine industry in Temecula in southern California. Not limited in range like the blue green sharpshooter, this modern locust could wreak havoc here also. After 160 years of dealing with disasters though, one has a feeling the Napa wine industry will be around for a long time.

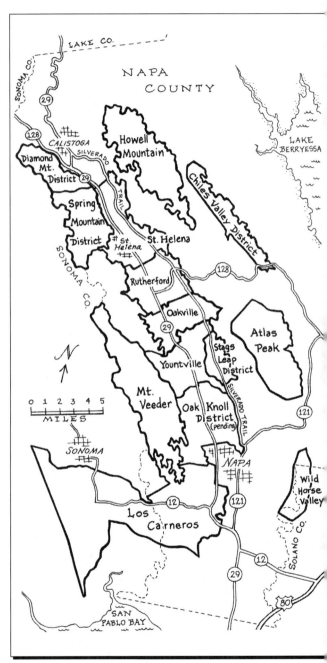

The wine appellations of the Napa Valley

Orientation—Learning the Lay of the Land

To facilitate an easy orientation to our subject, we have divided the county into four basic regions:

South Valley, locally referred to as Down-Valley—A maritime region near San Pablo Bay with cool, fog-shrouded mornings and generally warm, sunny afternoons in the summer. This area includes the famed Napa/Sonoma Los Carneros appellation, and is planted to early ripening Pinot Noir and Chardonnay.

Mid-Valley—The Yountville, Oakville and Rutherford area is the perfect place for Cabernet Sauvignon.

North Valley, locally referred to as Up-Valley—An area of intense summer heat that lends itself to the planting of later-ripening varietals like Zinfandel.

Eastern Hills and Valleys—From the Wild Horse Valley in the south to Howell Mountain in the north, the east county is home to a scenic patchwork of microclimates and unique growing regions.

■ About the Weather and Seasons

In the interest of best planning and enjoyment of your visit, we'll provide a summary of the weather and seasons. For the most part, Napa County has a moderate climate with some variation ranging from the marine-influenced south, with cool, occasionally foggy mornings, to the northern valley where it can be very hot and dry in the summer.

Considering the many moods of Mother Nature, we suggest a sweater, windbreaker, and sunscreen in the dry season, April through October. Our wet, or winter, season runs from November through March, and heavier clothing, rain gear, and yes, sunscreen, are recommended.

Picnics can be enjoyed year-round with some truly exceptional days tucked in between the wintertime Pacific rainstorms and the frosty mornings.

For up-to-date weather, pick up a copy of our excellent local newspaper, ***The Napa Register***, or visit them online at **www.napanews.com.**

■ Where To Stay

All the points of interest discussed in this book are within easy driving distance of anywhere in the San Francisco Bay Area and Marin or Sonoma counties. The Napa Valley is a perfect day trip, and it's even more fun as a holiday destination.

You'll find a full range of lodging choices organized by region in **Appendix B: Where to Stay**. You may also want to refer to **Appendix A: Getting Here/Mode of Travel** as you plan your adventure. **Chapter 10: Heading In/Heading Out** also has some helpful information for your trip planning and lodging in our neighboring counties.

■ Camping

Double your enjoyment of the Wine Country by combining your picnics with a peaceful slumber in the great outdoors. Napa County has a number of wonderful campgrounds, and the mild climate entices campers throughout the long season. Even the dead of winter offers pleasant camping if you're prepared.

In summer, especially on weekends, you will probably need a reservation. For a list of park choices and how to contact them, see Campgrounds in **Appendix B**. For private campgrounds in the area, please consult the Yellow Pages.

Legacy of Old Stones

Lucky for us there were and continue to be folks working with stone in the Napa Valley. Beautiful old stonework is one of the scenic wonders of this agricultural paradise. As a running theme throughout the book, we'll identify the details and histories of the Valley's historic stone bridges, buildings and utilitarian agricultural structures. The story of the stones is the story of harmonious living with what the land has to offer. Lovely stonework exemplifies Napa Valley style.

Old dry stackwork—Napa County

In the years between 1860 and 1910, many families who came from northern Italy and the Italian-speaking parts of Switzerland made Napa Valley their home. These people, long accustomed to building with stone, found that their stonemason's skills were in great demand. Grand old stone structures were built to house the wineries, trade shops, and even farm animals associated with a booming agriculture-based economy.

In the years following the discovery of gold in the Sierra Foothills, the economy expanded throughout northern California resulting in a severe shortage of labor. Coinciding with this boom time half a world away, China was experiencing floods, famine and economic hardship. Chinese men emigrated in great numbers to work in the Napa Valley. They provided the sweat and skill as contract labor crews on most of the historic stone structures including the numerous stone bridges that remain as functional and graceful evidence of a bygone era.

I Finally Heard the Laughter Up in Michigan

Stan Giedsic taught Smokey how to work with the fieldstones. That was back in the 1950s. Smokey taught Jeff, and Jeff started teaching me. I was an enthusiastic student back in the early 1970s, but my enthusiasm for the work was short-lived.

Smokey and Jeff, on the other hand, are still at it, still creating new monuments to their most ancient craft. They live in the hardwood and rock-strewn pasture country at the tip of Michigan's Lower Peninsula, an inspiring yet demanding place to try and make a living.

Back in the days before Paul Bunyan came to the North Woods, the vagaries of Mother Nature's climatic moods caused great sheets of ice to scour the hard granite lands above the Great Lakes. As the ice moved slowly south, it caught up an amazingly diverse collection of rocks. Industriously, the ice milled the rock into the beautiful, multi-colored, smooth boulders, fieldstones, and gravels that we find at the top of the mitt today.

All this free building material was unceremoniously left behind to bedevil the farmer folks and homesteaders who claimed the northern stump lands in the years after Paul and Babe the Blue Ox had managed to remove all the original tall, stately pines.

In my youthful enthusiasm, after having worked with Jeff on the foundation and chimney for just one lovely, handcrafted outbuilding, I began to see a fortune in every stone pile, easy money in every pasture.

I began to blather on about elaborate split stone facades, grand fireplaces, retaining walls, foundations and entire structures built of native fieldstone. I mean, there were literally thousands of enormous stone piles all over that country, and they were pretty much all free for the asking. Free! Free stone.

I recall feeling a little giddy as I began to plot my course to a fieldstone construction empire.

Smokey and Jeff were mostly silent on the subject of my more grandiose approach to their trade. When I would excitedly report on all the great new stone resources I was scouting, they would just look at me a little bewildered and then exchange a sly smile over their mid-workday shots and beers.

Stan Giedsic was laughing up in heaven, up in stonemason's heaven, a wind-blown Valhalla reserved for the hearty few who managed to die with a stone hammer in their hands.

I didn't know Stan was laughing at the time, but Smokey and Jeff did! I just thought the laughter was the howl of September and the rattle of sleet on the window of the Lark's Lake Bar.

Smokey and Jeff knew better. They knew it was the portent of many long months of snow when the stone piles would be buried deep. They knew too that there was a season of mud on either side of the snowpack, and that all the really good laying and splitting stones were already standing proudly, snug in their mortar, testimony to all the generations of farmer/masons and gyppo backwoods contractors like themselves.

For months, Smokey, Jeff and the old-timers at the Lark's Lake Bar had been quietly observing me banging away at a growing mound of mostly useless stone out in my yard. I had been trying to value-add by splitting the stones cleanly down the center. I hammered myself stone-silly in the evenings with an odd, oversized five-dollar flea-market maul.

I kept at it most of one summer. Beyond the pay I had received for working with Jeff that season, I had managed to earn absolutely no extra money either setting or selling stones. It was more than a little embarrassing when I finally admitted my defeat over beers at the Lark's Lake Bar.

Smokey smiled at me kindly. Jeff bought me a whiskey.

I found out about Stan Giedsic's laughter the hard way. There is a whole lot more to the craft than meets the eye. The work of a fieldstone mason is no picnic!

Bennet Bridge, Calistoga

2
The Traveling Picnicker

From wherever you wake up in Napa County, a pleasant hour of shopping will reward you with a tasty and economical prelude to the day's travels. The details of where to shop locally are laid out in **Chapter 3: Shopping for Your Picnic**. Before you head out to buy the food and beverages, however, you'll want to make sure you have the picnic gear you need. If you don't, you'll want to add a few things to your shopping list. Then you'll want to plan your means of transportation to the actual picnics. The second part of this chapter provides tips on how you might leave the car parked for the day and explore the Valley's picnic locations using a bicycle, motorcycle or limousine.

■ Picnic Paraphernalia

Gear for the successful picnic tourist can be as simple as a Swiss Army knife, tin cups and plates. You can also go to the extreme: full-dress basket, cooler, Coleman stove, folding chairs and table kit that might be best hauled about in a big shiny new SUV or van. Whatever your choice, here are the basics that pack easily into a daypack to go on your back or a basket to go into the car.

basket or day pack

small tablecloth and/or picnic blanket

luncheon-size plates (enamel-ware is nice)

larger plate or platter for serving

Tupperware-type bowl, large enough to toss four salads, with a good sealing lid

forks, spoons, butter knife

sturdy nesting glasses

2 tea or dish towels to wrap the glasses

corkscrew

simple, old-fashioned can opener

small, all-purpose camp or cook's knife with blade guard

small wood cutting board, 5"x 8" is all you need

cloth or paper napkins

oyster knife (optional)

small cooler (allows you an expanded menu)

We also carry the following easily transportable staples to prepare the picnic recipe items and to season prepared and deli-purchased foods:

small container of coarse salt

small pepper mill with black peppercorns

small jar of a favorite mustard

8-ounce bottle of extra-virgin olive oil

small, well-sealed bottle of red wine vinegar

bulb of fresh garlic

lemon or lime

♦

Our picnic kit has been accumulating for years, but if you want to toss one together on the spur of the moment, we suggest a trip to one of our local thrift stores. Or, we can recommend you visit one of the Valley's premier picnic outfitters:

■ Picnic Outfitters in the Napa Valley

Shackford's Kitchen Store
1350 Main Street
Napa 94559
226-2132
Without doubt, one of the best kitchen supply stores anywhere. Family owned and operated since 1975.

Campus Store at Greystone
2555 Main Street
St. Helena 94574
967-2309

For the enthusiastic professional or home chef, no visit to the Napa Valley would be complete without a stop at the Campus Store at Greystone. Housed in the grand old stone winery building that is now home to the Culinary Institute of America's West Coast campus, the store features 3,000 square feet of picnic gear, books, merchandise and food ingredients.

Dean & DeLuca Market
607 South St. Helena Highway
St. Helena 94574
967-9980

Astonishing selection and quality. Fresh fruits, cheeses, meats, wine (lots of 375 milliliter bottles, perfect for picnics), picnic supplies, fresh sandwiches daily, and a nice selection of first-rate picnic baskets and gear.

■ Limousine Touring

One deluxe way to tour the Napa Valley is to hire a limousine for your party and travel from winery to winery and other stops in style. It's the expensive option, but it comes complete with a designated driver and de facto tour guide. Nearly three dozen limousine services serve the Napa Valley. To find out more about this choice, look in the Yellow Pages of the local phone book under "Limousine." We recommend that if you do choose to travel by limo, you call ahead to the wineries you plan to visit to schedule your arrival times since some wineries don't permit unscheduled limo stops.

■ Bicycle Touring

Cycling offers a great way to see the Wine Country. Here are some rental opportunities, repair shops and tour companies that will help make your visit safe and fun. Do keep in mind that bike travel and extensive wine drinking are not a very good combination, as appealing as the idea might be.

NAPA

Bicycle Trax
796 Soscol Avenue
Napa 94559
258-8729

Napa Valley Bike Tours and Rentals / Napa Valley Cyclery
4080 Byway East (at Trower Avenue)
Napa 94558
255-3377

ST. HELENA

St. Helena Cyclery
1156 Main Street
St. Helena 94574
963-7736

CALISTOGA

Getaway Wine Country Bicycle Tours & Rentals
1117 Lincoln Avenue
Calistoga 94515
942-0332 or 800-499-2453

Palisades Mountain Sport
1330 Gerard Street
Calistoga 94515
942-9687

■ Motorcycle Touring

Some of Napa County's winding back roads are a motorcyclist's dream come true, but only if you're used to that kind of two-wheeling. Remember that California has a mandatory helmet law for both driver and rider. If you'd like to rent a motorcycle or bring your own for your Napa County tour, see the listings below.

Reed's Custom Cycles
674 Soscol Avenue
Napa 94559
256-3326
Repairs and service for Harleys.

Napa Valley Classics
820 Third Street
Napa 94559
253-8185
Large selection of used motorcycles.

Parriott Motors
1027 Pope Street
St. Helena 94574
963-1316 or 963-3190
Napa Valley's only Honda dealer.

■ Harley Davidson Rentals

Mike Nieman, the affable owner of Nieman's Auto Repair, has as a growing sideline a small fleet of beautiful Harleys that he would be happy to rent for your holiday puttering about in the Wine Country.

If you've ever dreamed of roaring through a slice of your life astride classic American iron, but have not yet bothered to buy your own, Mike offers the opportunity to indulge the fantasy.

Nieman's Motorcycle Rentals
1132 Main Street
St. Helena 94574
963-4618
www.niemansrental.com

Eagle Rider American Classic Rentals
1060 Bryant Street
San Francisco, CA 94103
888-390-4600
www.eaglerider.com

Rent a Harley in San Rafael
777 E. Francisco Blvd.
San Rafael, CA 94901
415-927-4464

3
Shopping for Your Picnic

There's no better way to get to know a neighborhood than by visiting the local grocers, bakers and farmers markets. Whether you plan to stay a day, a week or a lifetime, the real heart of the Napa Valley can be found as you shop for your afternoon picnic. Often your best wine-pairing and picnic hideaways come graciously with a bit of local gossip and your sandwich order, if you're open to it. The pleasant hour you might spend with curbside chit-chat and inquiries about a market vendor's multi-hued tomatoes could reveal the human landscape sometimes lost to lunch reservations and a tightly packed tour schedule.

This chapter is about encouraging you to slow down and smell the baked goods, taste the cheeses, and feast your eyes and ears in the marketplace.

THE FOODS

■ Bread and Bakers

Alexis Baking Company (ABC)
1517 Third Street
Napa 94559
258-1827
Open daily 6:30 a.m. to 6 p.m.
Alexis provides a vertical menu of breads, salads, desserts in equal measure.

Sciambra-Passini French Bakery
685 South Freeway Drive
Napa 94558
252-3072
Family-owned and operated wholesale business

for 21 years. You can find their products in grocery stores throughout the Valley.

Butter Cream Bakery
2297 Jefferson Street
Napa 94559
255-6700
Cafe open daily 5:30 a.m. to 5 p.m., bakery open until 8 p.m.
Since 1948, serving its famous home-style breakfasts and lunches.

San Marco Espresso and Bake Shop
1408 Lincoln Avenue
Calistoga 94515
942-0714
Open daily, 7 a.m. to 9 p.m. in winter, 6:30 a.m. to 10 p.m. in summer.
This tiny confectioner offers a mountain of goodies, including Italian pastry, carrot cake, brownies, and a dozen kinds of cookies. Birthday and wedding cakes to order.

Model Bakery
1357 Main Street
St. Helena 94574
963-8192
Open 6 a.m. to 6 p.m. Tuesday through Saturday, 8 a.m. to 4 p.m. Sunday. Closed Monday.
Great picnic sandwiches, pizetta, and sweets. Specializing in hand-formed, hearth-baked bread (over a dozen kinds) using only stone-ground organic flours.

Schat's Bakkerij
1353 Lincoln Avenue
Calistoga 94515
942-0777
Open 6 a.m. to 10 p.m. Friday and Saturday, 6 to 6 Sunday through Thursday, except closed Tuesday.
Co-owner Jan was part of a team that won the prestigious La Coupe du Monde de la Boulangerie competition in 1999 held in Paris. The original Schat's began in the Netherlands, now with individually owned and operated bakeries also in Bishop, Mammoth and Ukiah.

■ Cheese Makers

Lovely, locally produced, handcrafted cheeses are one of the basic complements to world-class Napa Valley wines. Cheese and winemaking go hand-in-hand, both being living products shepherded to the table by artisans skilled in ancient old-world crafts. The following is a brief introduction to Napa's foremost goat dairy and a number of other Northern California cheese makers whose products are available throughout the Valley.

Goat's Leap Dairy
3321 St. Helena Highway
St. Helena 94574
963-2337
Barbara and Rex Backus are currently making four distinctive true farmhouse cheeses from the milk of La Mancha goats:

Sumi—An attractive ashed flat-topped cheese encased in white mold with a nice, creamy texture.

Kiku—Barbara and Rex describe this rare seasonal cheese as a "mysterious puck robed in a sauvignon blanc-doused fig leaf." Delicious.

Carmela—A firm, six-pound wheel dusted with paprika. This one is best aged for a full year.

Goat's Leap Fresh Wheels—A great classic chèvre.

Skyhill Napa Valley Farms
2431 Patrick Road
Napa 94558
255-4800, 800-567-4628
Handmade goat milk cheeses and yogurt from their own herd of Nubian goats.

■ Other Northern California Cheese Makers

Northern California is home to literally herds of dairy goats, cows and sheep. Winter rains refresh miles of rolling coastal grasslands and snug valleys. The following is a brief introduction to some of our favorite cheese makers and their products. Most of these cheeses are available at several locations in the Napa Valley.

Bellwether Farms
Valley Ford 94972
778-0774, 888-527-8606
www.bellwethercheese.com
Cheese maker Cindy Callahan produces a variety of extraordinary cheeses from both Jersey cow and sheep milk. Keep your eye out for these favorites:

Toscano—Aged sheep-milk cheese

Caciotta—A young Toscano

Pepato—Aged Toscano with black peppercorns

San Andreas—Semi-soft sheep-milk cheese

Ricotta—Fresh sheep-milk cheese

Carmody—A buttery, Jersey-cow milk cheese, aged four to six weeks

Crescenza—A beautifully rich and tart young cheese in the Italian style of Lombardy

Laura Chenel's Chèvre
Sonoma 95476
996-4477
Conveniently packaged for picnics and available at most grocers, this mild goat-milk cheese is great with olive salad on a baguette.

Redwood Hill Farm
5480 Thomas Road
Sebastopol 95472
823-8250
www.redwoodhill.com
Two hundred and fifty dairy goats, and each one has a name. Happy herds make for great cheese. Our favorite is their small, French-style crottin, perfect for a picnic or two. They also make yogurt, fresh chèvre, feta, and a delicious Camellia, a Camembert-style mold-ripened cheese.

Joe Matos Cheese
3669 Llano Road
Santa Rosa 95407
584-5283
Just east of Sebastopol off Highway 12 in Sonoma County, the Matos family make a delicious aged cheese from the milk of their Holstein cows. It's called St. George and can't be beat as an accompaniment to a simply-dressed salad of sweet and bitter greens.

Cypress Grove Chèvre
4600 Dows Prairie Road
McKinleyville 95519
839-3168
From up north in Humboldt County comes goat-milk cheese that will take you back to France. These folks do a terrific job with both fresh and ripened cheeses. We really enjoy their Humboldt Fog.

Bodega Goat Cheese
P.O. Box 223
Bodega 94922
876-3483
www.bodegagoatcheese.com
This small family farm makes traditional South American fresh country-style cheeses, as well as quesocabrero, a very tasty, 60-days aged Manchego-style raw milk cheese.

Marin French Cheese Company
7500 Redhill Road
Petaluma 94952
762-6001
www.marinfrenchcheese.com
Look for conveniently packaged and delicious Rouge et Noir brand Camembert, Brie, breakfast

cheese and tangy schloss cheese. Available at most grocers, or visit the factory in Sonoma County on the way to Point Reyes National Seashore.

Vella Cheese Company of Sonoma

315 Second Street East
P.O. Box 191
Sonoma 95476
800-848-0505
www.vellacheese.com

Purveyors of fine handmade cheese since 1931. Look for Bear Flag brand cheese at most local grocers and delis. We are particularly fond of their Asiago and special select dry Monterey jack.

When visiting over in Sonoma, stop in to see the various cheeses being made. Informal tours start at 12:30 p.m., Monday through Thursday.

Pt. Reyes Original Blue

415-663-8880
www.pointreyescheese.com

The Giacomini family has a simple mission on their lovely dairy set in the splendid coastal rangelands alongside Tomales Bay: to produce the nation's premier brand of high-end blue table cheese. From your first taste of their product, you'll agree that they are well on their way to meeting their goal.

Clover-Stornetta Farms

91 Lakeville Highway
Petaluma 94954
800-821-3072, 778-8448
All kinds of dairy products. Fresh, wholesome and available everywhere.

All these lovely handmade and often seasonal cheeses can be found throughout the Napa Valley in the groceries and on restaurant menus. If you're interested in ordering a favorite northern California cheese online, visit **www.sonomapicnic.com** for links to all the makers mentioned above.

The following is a list of locations with particularly tasty cheese selections:

(Down-valley to up-valley:)
Copia (See page 97)
Vallerga's Markets (page 45)
The Soda Canyon Store (page 46)

Oakville Grocery (page 47)
V. Sattui Winery (page 77)
The Napa Valley Olive Oil Co. (page 47)
Sunshine Foods (page 49)
Palisades Market (page 50)

■ Farm-Fresh Produce

Herbs of the Napa Valley
1832 Sulphur Springs Road
St. Helena 94574
963-7096
Products found in the finer Valley establishments.

Forni-Brown Vegetables
900 Foothill Blvd.
Calistoga 94515
942-6123
They sell mostly wholesale, but check out their plant sale in the early spring.

■ Farmers Markets

The farmers markets in the Valley provide your best source of local seasonal produce, flowers, honey and farm-crafted products. The market season generally runs from May to October. We eagerly await the first market days of spring for fresh flowers or the early salad mixes and greens. Market days are also pleasant social occasions.

Napa Valley Farmers Market
In the parking lot behind Kaiser/Lui/Lee Building, between Main and West Streets, Napa
252-7142, 265-8602
Tuesdays 7:30 a.m. to noon, May through October.

Napa Downtown Chefs Market
First Street from Main to Franklin Streets, Napa
257-0322
Fridays 4 p.m. to 9 p.m., May through September.
Food, music, cooking demos, more.

Yountville Farmers Market
Vintage 1870 at Compadres, Yountville
944-0904
Wednesdays 4 p.m. to 8 p.m., June through October.

St. Helena Farmers Market
South parking lot at Crane Park, St. Helena
265-8602
Fridays 7:30 a.m. to 11:30 a.m., May through October.

Calistoga Farmers Market
At the old Gliderport, just past Palisades Market on the east side of Calistoga
Saturday mornings 8:30 a.m. to 12:30 p.m., June through September.
Produce, coffee, local pastry, and a hands-on artwork booth for children.

■ Olives and Olive Oil

Napa Valley is particularly well-suited to the production of distinctive and much-sought-after olive oils. Olive oil production is a natural complement to grape-growing and winemaking as the trees thrive in the same Mediterranean clime as do the vines. The fruit of the olive trees ripens slowly on the heels of the grape harvest. Many wineries and ranches are now taking advantage of a legacy of olive trees thoughtfully planted sometimes well over a hundred years ago.

Napa Valley Olive Oil Manufacturing Company
835 Charter Oak Avenue
St. Helena 94574
963-4173
Open daily.
See page 98—Great Picnic Places

Long Meadow Ranch Winery
St. Helena 94574
963-4555

Ultra-premium extra virgin olive oil from organically grown olives. Their Prato lungo was named Best "California olive oil" and "top recommendation" by **Buyers Guide to Olive Oil.** *Available on the internet or by calling direct.*

St. Helena Olive Oil Company
8576 St. Helena Highway
Rutherford 94573
967-1003
www.sholiveoil.com
Open daily.

This is a great stop along a great food and wine road. You get the feeling as you savor the lovely oils and house-made vinegars at the St. Helena Olive Oil Company that there just might be a little history in the making at this bustling production and retail facility. The owners have a wonderful sense of style along with an obvious commitment to producing the highest quality oil and vinegar for your picnic salads. They also invite you to inquire about bringing or joining a group educational presentation on the sensory evaluation of olive oils. They sell picnic supplies too.

M. Turrigiano & Company
1407 Earl Street
Napa 94559
253-0519

Michael Turrigiano produces very limited quantities of a delicious pale green olive oil from groves in the Pope Valley. His unique handmade ceramic vessels were inspired by an old found bottle and perfectly complement the oil within by protecting it from the degrading effects of heat and light.

Look for Michael's Oil at:
Vanderbilt & Co. in St. Helena
Merryvale Vineyards in St. Helena
Niebaum-Coppola Winery in Rutherford
Oakville Grocery in Oakville

**Recipe for Marinated Anchovies from
Michael Turrigiano**
Bruschetta con Acciughe

1. Combine ingredients and let stand overnight at room temperature:
   - **1 bunch Italian parsley, minced**
   - **1 clove garlic, finely minced**
   - **1 11 oz. jar imported Italian anchovies, drained**
   - **1 cup M. Turrigiano Olive Oil, plus more as needed to completely cover anchovies**

2. For the bruschetta, slice a good crunchy rustic loaf of bread into ½ inch slices, brush with Michael's Olive Oil, and grill or bake until nicely toasted.

3. Serve the anchovies in a bowl at room temperature with the bruschetta on the side. They make a wonderful accompaniment to a summer salad or a hearty winter soup picnic.

■ Olives for the Table

Although we have many opportunities to enjoy the oil of local olives, locally cured olives themselves are

Swartz Creek Bridge on Aetna Springs Road

a rare treat reserved for those who know someone who is making them at home. I hope this situation will change in the near future, because a quiet demand is building in California for California olives cured in the traditional European and North African ways. Keep your eyes peeled and until that happy day, we love to make do with the amazing diversity of imported olives available throughout the Valley.

■ Grapeseed Oil

Long a traditional and healthful staple in European and South American kitchens, the oil made from grape seeds reserved from the winemaking and cold-pressed is new to the neighborhood.

Napa Valley Grapeseed Oil is produced on the premises of Rutherford Grove Winery, 1673 St. Helena Highway (Highway 29) between St. Helena and Rutherford, 963-0544.
www.rutherfordgrove.com/grapeseed.html.
Stop in and say hello!

■ Seafood

Vallerga's Markets
All stores open daily.
3385 Solano Avenue, Napa 94558, 253-2621
301 First Street, Napa 94559, 253-1666
1525 Imola Avenue, Napa 94558, 253-2622

Omega 3 Seafood
1740 Yajome Street
Napa 94559
257-3474
Retail market open Tuesday through Saturday.
Their wholesale business provides fresh seafood to many of the Napa Valley's best restaurants. Specialize in cold and hot smoked Atlantic salmon, sturgeon, and salmon paté.

Sunshine Foods
1117 Main Street
St. Helena 94574
963-7070
Open daily.
Up-Valley's best selection of fresh fish.

Keller's Market
1320 Main Street
St. Helena 94574
963-2114
Open daily.
Fresh fish at Ernie's meats.

Cal Mart
1491 Lincoln Avenue
Calistoga 94515
942-6271
Open daily.
Full-service meat market has fresh fish daily.

■ Picnic Meats and Sausages

This section offers a note on food safety. **Napa Valley Picnic** does not address any serious cooking or barbecuing. The guide is meant to encourage the casual traveler to patronize our fine local delis, farm markets and grocers. When it comes to meat or poultry items for your picnic menus, we suggest you purchase fully cooked products. If you buy them hot, eat them hot and promptly. If you purchase fully cooked cold sausages, roast chicken or chicken salads, keep them cold and eat them cold. Of course you may reheat precooked and chilled meats, fish or poultry over a twig fire (see page 66) or charcoal. Avoid the hazard of buying that gorgeous, crisp rotisserie chicken, then making a couple of wine-tasting stops before you eat it. Purchase hot food with a specific picnic stop in mind and get right to the business of lunch.

Gerhard's Napa Valley Sausages (wholesale)
901 Enterprise Way
Napa 94558
252-4116
Look for Gerhard's fully cooked sausages at most of the Valley's grocery and specialty shops. These handcrafted local sausages make for tasty picnics, hot or cold, and you can choose from over a dozen varieties to suit the season. Owner Gerhard Twele of Germany was in the restaurant business for decades before starting his own company. All sausages are made without MSG, fillers, preservatives or artificial flavors.

Keller's Market Meat Counter
1320 Main Street
St. Helena 94574
963-9608

Right downtown on Main Street, this old-time grocery has a gem of a meat department featuring wonderful homemade fresh sausages and some of the best sandwiches in the Valley. They usually cook up a batch of sausage every day for sandwich specials, and if you call a day ahead they will be happy to cook up a few for your picnic.

Sunshine Foods
1117 Main Street
St. Helena 94574
936-7070

In addition to being a world-class grocery store, the folks at Sunshine offer some really good freshly cooked foods off an aromatic and smoky barbecue set up outside the kitchen door.

THE SHOPS

■ Down-Valley Shopping

Vallerga's Markets
South Napa 94558: Riverpark Village at Imola Avenue,
  deli 253-8780
East Napa 94559: 301 First Street at Silverado Trail,
  deli 253-2780
North Napa 94558: Riverwood Shopping Center,
  Solano Avenue at Jefferson Street, deli 253-7846
www.vallergas.com

With these locations, Vallerga's Markets are good stops for stocking up on picnic supplies. The delis have a good selection of freshly prepared hot entrees and soups for winter wine-tasting adventures. The East Napa store is a particularly handy location that includes the unusual feature of a post office, and it's just down the street from the grounds of Copia on the lovely oxbow of the Napa River (page 113).

Golden Carrot Natural Foods
1621 West Imola Avenue
Napa 94559
224-3117
Open daily.
Bulk herb selection, some fresh foods, and an entire wall of vitamins and supplements.

Optimum Natural Foods and Products
633 Trancas Street
Napa 94558
224-1514
Open daily.
They offer a variety of vitamins and supplements, natural cosmetics and body care, bulk herbs, homeopathic remedies, green foods and energy products, refrigerated items and much more.

Soda Canyon Store
4006 Silverado Trail
Napa 94558
252-0285
Open daily.
A landmark for half a century, the newly remodeled store features a deli, gourmet foods, espresso bar, wine bar, and outside seating at the picnic area overlooking the historic Soda Canyon Bridge.

Old Soda Canyon Bridge

■ Mid Valley Shopping

Ranch Market Too
6498 Washington Street
Yountville 94599
944-2662
Open 365 days a year.

The main place for groceries in beautiful downtown Yountville. Sandwich and coffee bar is a sit down affair. It's a center for locals, with video rentals and a copy machine. Picnic supplies too.

Oakville Grocery Company
7856 St. Helena Highway
Oakville 94582
944-8802
Upscale shopping in a once downscale country store. Great sandwiches, cheeses, olives and wine

Sycamores near Oakville Cross Road

selection. We recommend their vegetarian sandwich with local Skyhill chèvre.

La Luna Market
1153 Rutherford Cross Road
Rutherford 94573
963-3211
Open daily.
A local secret serving up lunchtime mega-burritos.

■ Up-Valley Shopping
Napa Valley Olive Oil Company
835 Charter Oak Avenue
St. Helena 94574
963-4173
continued on page 49

Napa Valley olives

Baccalá Flashback

It did not matter that no Italians at all were working in the Mario's kitchen. Mario's was still a very Italian restaurant in Detroit—an old-school Italian dinnerhouse—and it did not matter that the owner was not Italian either. She had come into possession of the place by putting in enough years with an Italian to have it awarded to her in the divorce settlement.

Hardly anyone ever mentioned the former Italian management. It was quite evident, though, that everyone had paid attention during the Italian's tenancy. All the dishes—the pizzas, spaghetti, big shrimp, and veal—were prepared faithfully in the Italian way and with the traditional and imported ingredients. It was my job, way back then in the years following the Summer of Love, to go fetch the special Italian ingredients from a very special kind of market.

In those days I had not yet been to Europe, and even though I was quite interested in food and cooking, my idea of a grocery store was something along the line of what we used to call a supermarket—bright, spotless, economical, and with a crushing antiseptic, pre-packaged soullessness.

My first mission to the Italian grocery was an eye opener! I had been sent to get some salt cod for a special dish, and what I encountered lingers not so much in my mind as on the nose—a heady aroma of cured meats, cheeses, dried mushrooms and salted fish. Everything was heaped in baskets, stacked like cordwood, or hanging from the rafters of the old barn of a structure that seemed out of place within the context of its Detroit space and time.

That place had a reality about it that inspired me to think more deeply about food, where it comes from, and its journey to our tables. That Italian grocery had some serious soul!

Nowadays I enjoy shopping at the Napa Valley Olive Oil Company not only for the great selection of foods, but also for a certain sense of psychic transport. The minute I walk through the door of this wonderfully real establishment, I find myself visiting my distant past and the days when baccalá—salt cod—was all new to me.

This classic and historic Italian grocery is a regular destination for the chefs of the North Bay for an incredible selection of uniquely Italian kitchen staples. It also is a place that always transports us, a portal to both the culinary past and future. A visit to St. Helena is not complete without a stop in here, because it's a great place to put together and enjoy a rustic picnic. (See page 98)

Dean & DeLuca
607 South St. Helena Highway
St. Helena 94574
967-9980
Open daily.
Absolutely top-shelf shopping with deluxe ingredients and picnic fare.

Cantinetta & Wine Bar at Tra Vigne
1050 Charter Oak Avenue
St. Helena 94574
963-8888
A great place for scrumptious picnic foods, whether you take them away or eat them here. Savor the flavors of Italy and the Napa Valley with an educational tour of the many wines offered by the two-ounce tasting while you choose your lunch from the handsome display cases.

Sunshine Foods
1117 Main Street
St. Helena 94574
963-7070
Open daily.
Our local favorite has fresh soups and sandwiches daily, great produce, great cheese selection, olive bar, bread baked every day, best seafood in town, sushi bar, meat counter, picnic supplies and regular food too.

Keller's Market
1320 Main Street
St. Helena 94574
963-2114
Open daily.
A classic old-time grocery with a thoughtful mix of picnic staples, a superb meat market, seafood, and sandwiches made daily.

Nature Select Foods
1080 Main Street
St. Helena 94574
967-8545
Open daily.

St. Helena's full-service health food store has all the products you've come to expect in a quality store.

Palisades Market
1506 Lincoln Avenue
Calistoga 94515
942-9549
Open daily.

This book and our ideas about creating a practical culinary guide to the Napa Valley began over a memorable and tasty picnic at the Palisades Market. It's often the first and last stop on our travels, and a great place to create your own picnics from all the good things that come out of the kitchen and cold cases.

Calistoga Natural
1426 Lincoln Avenue
Calistoga 94515
942-5822
Open daily.

Kelley's completely refurbished store is a must-see, now with a full-service lunch bar.

Mitchell's Drive-In Grocery
1102 Tubbs Lane
Calistoga 94515
942-4446

A country convenience store on Highway 128, a mile north of town.

Wapoo Market
207 Wapoo Avenue
Calistoga 94515
942-4909

Get a taste of Mexico at this tiny neighborhood groceria. Colorful piñatas hanging from the ceiling are for sale as well as traditional Mexican foods and drinks. Good selection of fresh fruit out front.

Cal Mart
1491 Lincoln Avenue
Calistoga 94515
942-6271
Open daily.

Calistoga's only full-service grocery has sandwiches made daily, a vast selection of fine cheeses and breads, seafood, meats and poultry, olive bar, bulk foods, and fresh produce,including organic.

4
Picnic Menus

For the traveler, options for picnic menus depend on where you shop, so we'll suggest menus with specific stops in mind.

We present the menus in the form of a recipe. Use the method as a guide for shopping, but do shop around and keep an eye out for seasonal amendments or substitutions.

■ Palisades Market Picnic Menu for Spring and Summer

Chef/Owner Victoria Gott of Palisades Market has kindly suggested this menu for a simple one-stop shopping Calistoga-area picnic.

Menu:

Olives de Provence—black olives with herbs in olive oil.

Goat's Leap fresh goat's milk cheese—one of the Valley's best-kept secrets. (See page 35)

Sour baguette from Artisan Bakery with a great crunchy crust.

Caesar salad or chicken Caesar salad—unique and delicious.

Bridge near the Palisades

Palisades Ding-Dong—a world-class dessert of rich chocolate cake, sweet creamy filling and chocolate granache!

You can enjoy your picnic on the patio behind the Market with a nice bottle of Joel Gott wines (Sauvignon Blanc or Zinfandel), with a terrific view up-valley to the Palisades mountain range.

Some of Victoria's other favorite picnic spots are:

Pioneer Park in Calistoga (see page 88).
Heather Oaks Park in Calistoga (see page 88).
Cuvaison Winery in Calistoga (see page 82).

■ Stonemason's Picnic

This menu and recipe celebrate summer's first local tomatoes and the tail end of artichoke season, or summer's last local tomatoes and the start of autumn artichoke season.

Menu:

Stonemason's Artichokes (see recipe, next page)

Salad of tomatoes, cucumbers, sweet pepper and fresh basil leaves

Mixed olives for the table

Bellwether Farms Crescenza, a fresh Jersey cow's milk cheese

Model Bakery bread

Fresh fruit and roasted almonds

This menu requires a little cooking if you happen to find yourself in a place with a kitchen. If not, substitute a jar of marinated artichokes.

Method:

Model Bakery for fresh baked bread.

St. Helena Farmers Market for salad fixings and fruit.

Sunshine Foods for jumbo artichokes or marinated artichokes, cheese and almonds.

This is a good picnic to enjoy in the presence of historic handcut stone at tiny Nichelini Winery in Sage Canyon, an out-of-the-way winery founded by an Italian stonemason in the days following the Gold Rush. It's a bit of a drive, and they're only open on weekends, but the trip on Highway 128, the road to Lake Berryessa, is well worth the journey.

■ Stonemason's Artichokes

1. Choose two large fresh artichokes and prepare them as follows:
A. Cut ½ " away from the top and the stem. Trim the tips of each leaf with a pair of scissors.
B. Split the artichoke vertically and remove the choke with a spoon.
C. Soak the prepared halves in a bowl of cold water with the juice of ½ lemon added to it.
2. Saute briefly in a 12" heavy pan that is at least 2" deep and has a good, close-fitting lid:

   ¼ cup olive oil
   8 cloves garlic, rough chopped
   2 Tbls. fresh rosemary leaves
   1 tsp. red chili flakes

3. Before the garlic has a chance to color, place the artichokes in the pan, split-side down, and add, in the following order:
   1 cup water
   1 lemon (squeeze lemon over the artichoke and include the rinds)
   ½ tsp. kosher salt

4. Bring to a boil over high heat, cover, and braise 10 minutes.
5. Remove the lid, check for tenderness (they may need another minute or two with the lid on), then boil away any remaining liquid and carefully brown the contents of the pan.
6. Remove the artichokes to a nice platter and arrange split-side up. Dress them with all the oil and caramelized bits from the pan, plus the juice of ½ lemon, some lemon wedges, and a pinch of salt.

■ Denise's Favorite V. Sattui Picnic

Denise has worked at V. Sattui Winery for years, and she kindly suggested the following picnic:

Menu:
Roasted garlic with baguette and cambazola or
Point Reyes Blue Cheese

Apples and pears

Pasta salad

Famous Gulf prawns in mustard sauce

Don't forget to look in the pastry case

Method:
Park, shop, taste wine, and enjoy! V. Sattui Winery has it all in a lively and lovely setting. Denise suggests a bottle of Gamay Rouge. Suzanne's Vineyard Zin is another excellent choice, or you can choose your own favorite with a little help from the very friendly and knowledgeable tasting bar staff.

■ Country French-Style Harvest Picnic

Menu:
Paté

Goat's Leap cheeses

Salad of local mixed greens dressed simply with the juice of wine or table grapes

Local olive oil, a pinch of salt, and black pepper

Della Fattoria bread and butter

Cornichons and olives for the table

Ripe figs

Method:
This menu calls for one-stop shopping at Oakville Grocery in Oakville. They offer a terrific selection of patés and all the seasonal offerings from our friends at Goat's Leap. You can ask for some mixed greens at the deli counter, and pick up a bottle of M. Turrigiano olive oil, which is delicious with

Della Fattoria bread, delivered hot out of the wood ovens daily after 2 p.m.

We might also suggest you make your way east on the Oakville Cross Road and head south on the Silverado Trail to Robert Sinskey Winery (see page 72) for a bottle of their lovely Vin Gris de Pinot Noir.

*Stonework at **Rudd Vineyards** on Oakville Cross Road*

■ Introduction to the Slow Food Movement

Think "in season and local." Think "traditional foods and tastes," then ponder the picnic menu possibilities available to us here in our California melting pot of wonderfully diverse culinary cultures. The International Slow Food Movement was founded in 1986 by a man in Italy. He decided to create an organization that could act as a positive counterpart to the global encroachment of fast life and fast food.

Slow Food is a global nonprofit organization dedicated to supporting and celebrating traditional foods, the pleasures of the table, and the quality of life. Slow Food is all about enjoying life. It's about taking the time to savor not only our meals and the company of our fellows, but also more fully embracing the community of farmers and artisans who provide the food for our table.

■ Trans-Valley Summer Slow Food Picnic

Menu:

Freshly baked bread from the Model Bakery

Summer Salad (see page 61)

Selection of local cheeses from V. Sattui Winery

Stone fruit and berries with Strauss Dairy cream and Marshall's Farm honey

Method (as you travel north to south):

1. Start your day with coffee, conversation, and a pastry hot out of the old brick ovens at the Model Bakery in St. Helena. Purchase a rustic crunchy loaf of bread to eat with your summer salad and local cheeses.

2. On any summer Friday, make your way to the St. Helena Farmers Market in Crane Park (open 7:30 a.m. to 11:30 a.m., see page 40). If it's a summer Saturday, visit the Calistoga Farmers Market, 8:30 a.m. to noon at the Gliderport (see page 40).

Sunshine Market, located on the southern end of downtown St. Helena at 1117 Main Street is a great place to shop any day of the week. They have a nice selection of fruit and vegetables with some good local and organic choices for your salad and dessert. Sunshine Market is also the place to pick up a pint of Strauss Organic Dairy cream in the old fashioned glass bottle. Don't sweat the $1 deposit on the bottle. The cream inside, from happy West Marin County cows, is more than worth it. If you don't get a chance to return the bottle, it makes a swell souvenir flower vase for casual picnics at home.

3. V. Sattui Winery at 1111 White Lane, just south of St. Helena off Highway 29, is a great place to stop for cheese. You'll find the very best selection of northern California farmstead cheeses as well as a cheerful and knowledgeable staff. Choose a goat's milk cheese for your salad and a small portion of two others, perhaps one made from cow's milk and one from the milk of sheep. At V. Sattui they'll be happy to help you choose.

4. Continue south to the St. Helena Olive Oil Company at 8576 Highway 29 in Rutherford to

sample house-pressed extra virgin olive oil and their own lovely wine vinegars. It's a fun, educational shop for your summer salad oil and vinegar, and you can purchase small bottles for your picnic basket. (See page 41)

5. The next stop is way down south in American Canyon by the Solano County line. Slow Food members Helene and Spencer Marshall welcome you to visit Marshall's Farm and the Flying Bee Ranch. Here you can sample and choose from many unique natural honeys. Each distinctive honey comes from hives that are located at specific local gardens, orchards and ranches where the bees forage among particular varieties and combinations of blossoms. Marshall's Farm is just off Highway 29 eight miles south of Napa. As you travel south on Highway 29, turn right onto Napa Junction Road, then take the first right onto Lombard Road. Look for the honey-colored buildings and the little red barn at the Flying Bee Ranch on the left.

Marshall's Farm
159 Lombard Road
American Canyon 94503
556-8088, 800-624-4637
www.marshallshoney.com
Open 10 a.m. to 6 p.m. Monday through Friday, 11 a.m. to 6 p.m. weekends.

For more information and links to the tasty world of Slow Food, visit the Slow Food feature at **www.sonomapicnic.com**

For your picnic, we might suggest that you take all your gathered delectables and head to the Carneros for a nice pairing with the wines of Madonna Estate/Mount St. John Cellars (see page 70).

Just travel six miles back north on Highway 29 and turn left onto Highway 12/121, then go about a mile and turn right onto the Old Sonoma Road.

■ Winter Picnic for Sunny Days

Menu:

Hot soup and crackers with Jimtown Chopped
Olive Spread

Deli sandwiches and pickles

Crisp apples and Vella Cheese Co. Bear Flag
brand Asiago or dry Monterey jack cheese

Method:

This is simple one-stop shopping for any of the Vallerga's Markets in Napa. They always have a pot of delicious hot soup on, and you can choose your crackers, Jimtown Chopped Olive Spread, pickles and crackers, as well as a nice piece of cheese.

With picnic delectables safely tucked in the hamper, we suggest you scoot south and west on Highway 12/121 and get to Madonna Estate/Mount St. John Winery before the soup cools off. This is a picnic that will go nicely with a bottle of Gewürztraminer under the winter naked grape arbor.

5
Recipes for Travelers

Here are a few recipes that you can prepare at the picnic table, on a blanket, or in your room at your lodging. Some of our most memorable meals have been prepared simply out of our picnic kit on trains, ferry decks and hotel balconies. Watching the world go by, passing the bread around, meeting new people, and conserving your travel funds makes for a great holiday.

■ Sauces and Dips

The following three basic accompaniments to your picnic menus are easy to prepare and keep for a few days if you're traveling with a small ice cooler.

Tzatziki
A refreshing dip for bread or accompaniment to roast chicken.
1. Peel, seed and finely dice:
   1 small cucumber
2. Place a paper napkin over the diced cucumber. With the palm of your hand, press as much juice out of the cucumber as you can. Get it dry—it may take two napkins.
3. Peel and mince very fine:
   1 small clove of garlic (about 1 teaspoon)
4. Combine in your salad bowl:
   8-oz. container plain yogurt (save the container)
   cucumber
   garlic
   1 Tbls. olive oil
   pinch of salt
5. Return as much of the Tzatziki as fits to the yogurt container and keep on ice for your next meal. Dip from what's left in the salad bowl with a nice loaf of crunchy bread.

You can omit or use more garlic according to
your taste. You may also keep your eyes out for the
wild fennel that seems to grow all over the county, or
fresh mint. Pinch a few sprigs if it seems
appropriate, mince the leaves and add to your
tzatziki for a pleasant change. Note on tzatziki: The
more flavorful the yogurt, the better the sauce! We
like Redwood Hill Farms brand.

Mayoli
(Cheater's Aioli)

*Not the real, authentic French deal, but still
delicious on sandwiches, or as a dip for fresh
vegetables and crisp romaine. Keep on ice in your
cooler and enjoy it over a weekend of picnics.*

*Note: When you purchase your jar of mayonnaise,
plan to use some of it plain, in tuna or chicken salad,
or on sandwiches, then you have room to build your
mayoli right in the jar.*

1. Remove and use ¼ of an 8-oz. jar of Best Foods
Real Mayonnaise®
2. Mince very fine:
    1 small clove of garlic
3. Combine in the mayonnaise jar:
    remaining mayonnaise
    minced garlic
    juice of ½ small lemon
4. Stir in with a fork:
    enough olive oil to fill the jar
    (approximately 2 Tbls.)

We like to dip leaves of crunchy romaine or
spinach while nibbling pocketknife shavings of
Bellwether Farms Toscano cheese. Use mayoli as you
would mayonnaise, on sandwiches or in salads. Add
capers, fresh minced tarragon leaves, or minced
anchovies for a delicious accompaniment to a
rotisserie chicken.

Fresh Tomato Condiment
(Salsa Cruda)

1. Combine in your salad bowl:

1 large tomato, diced (about 1 cup)
½ small garlic clove, minced fine
10 leaves fresh basil, cut or torn into small
    pieces
2 Tbls. olive oil

2. Season to taste with salt and freshly ground black pepper.

Tomatoes in season are one of the many pleasures of Napa County's farmers markets and roadside stands. Enjoy salsa cruda spooned onto chunks of fresh, country-style bread, or try topping this combination with little spoons of local goats-milk cheese.

When you're almost done with your spooning and topping, leave a smidgen of salsa in your bowl. Build a tasty salad by adding fresh greens, a splash of vinegar, and some olive oil.

Please do add capers and/or anchovies to your salsa cruda, or try some chopped imported olives or spring onion. Add fresh lime, cilantro and minced fresh jalapeño chili. Bring along a bag of corn chips—go wild! Save half a recipe of salsa cruda. Add some bits of leftover bread and a can of cooked white cannellini beans for a rustic treat.

■ Salads

The trick for a picnic chef is finding a way to wash your greens and vegetables. Of course, most markets now have washed mixed greens, salad mixes, sauté mixes, spinach leaves and romaine hearts, the basis of many wonderful salads and a convenient choice for the traveler. However, if you're washing your own fruits and vegetables, use your salad bowl and find water in your room, at gas stations, or at plaza and roadside drinking fountains. Wash your salad greens whole-head, shake dry and store in the salad bowl with the lid on. When preparing picnics at a winery that allows it, ask the tasting room staff about a place to wash your vegetables or a source of potable water.

Napa Valley Summer Salad
All the classic flavors of the summer garden are combined with a splash of lively red wine from the harvest past and the cold pressed oil of local olives.

1. Combine in your salad bowl:
   > **3 small vari-colored tomatoes, cut into chunks**
   > **1 small cucumber, peeled and cut into chunks**
   > **1 sweet pepper, seeded and cut into chunks**
   > **½ small sweet onion, sliced**
   > **½ bunch parsley, coarsely chopped**
   > **15 kalamata olives**
2. Dress with:
   > **3 Tbls. red wine**
   > **3 Tbls. (local) olive oil**
   > **1 Tbls. red wine vinegar**
3. Finish with:
   > **¼ lb. Goat's Leap Carmela cheese (if you can find it), cut in chunks, or any fresh local goats milk cheese, crumbled**
   > **A pinch of salt and black pepper**

Provençal Salad

Here's a take on the famous salad of Nice that is convenient for the traveler. The hard-cooked eggs in the classic salad can sometimes be replaced by deviled eggs from a deli counter, or you may skip them, or ask at your breakfast café for a couple of hard-boiled eggs to go.

1. Arrange on your serving plate:
   > **bed of mixed greens, or torn lettuce leaves**
   > **1 medium tomato, quartered**
   > **1 small cucumber, sliced**
   > **1 sweet pepper, seeded and sliced**
   > **2 hard-boiled or deviled eggs, quartered**
   > **1 small can white tuna, in large flakes**
   > **4 green onions, just trimmed**
   > **pinch of salt and freshly ground black pepper**
2. Garnish with:
   > **very tender raw green or wax beans, if available, and 12 imported black olives**
3. Dress with the artichokes and juice from one
   > **6 ½ -ounce jar of marinated artichoke hearts, and:**
   > **1 Tbls. red wine vinegar**

Take liberty with this salad, and make it a celebration of the season. In early spring, look for tiny asparagus or very fresh fava beans to shell and hull. Summer brings tiny carrots and squash to our markets and farm stands—shopping for this one is half the fun!

Salad Sandwich or Pan Bagnat

If you have some Provençal Salad left over, or plan to make extra, here is a portable meal for a sunset hike:

1. Cut a baguette or flat round loaf of bread in half and hollow out some of the interior to make room for the salad.
2. Spoon and arrange the salad in the hollow and dress with enough juice and oil to moisten but not soak through the bread.
3. Wrap in a plastic bag and keep cool for your evening adventure. Enjoy with a chilled bottle of local Sauvignon Blanc.

Salad of Seasonal Greens Vinaigrette

Fresh mixed tiny lettuces and greens are available almost all year long in most grocery stores. We like to purchase just what we need for one meal, and then get an extra bunch of arugula to add to and enhance the salad. Dress with this simple vinaigrette:

1. Combine:
> **1 small shallot, minced**
> **pinch of salt**
> **1 tsp. prepared mustard**
> **1 Tbls. red wine vinegar, or the juice of ½ lemon**
> **3 Tbls. olive oil**

2. Let this dressing sit for a few minutes to allow the shallot to mellow, and then whisk it with a fork and toss your salad. Pass the Chardonnay!

Chopped Salad

Here's a take on the classic Waldorf Salad fondly remembered from family gatherings that always featured a nice glazed ham and the sound of the aunties scolding mischievous, overly-amped children.

1. Combine in a salad bowl:
> **1 small head of iceberg or romaine lettuce, chopped**

1 large crisp apple, chopped
3 stalks celery, chopped
1 cup table grapes, split
¼ cup walnuts
¼ cup mayonnaise
1 Tbls. olive oil
1 Tbls. Meyer lemon juice

After you've enjoyed your chopped salad, you'll find yourselves in possession of a partial jar of mayonnaise and most of a bunch of celery. The following recipe is a suggestion to visit a farmers market to assemble the ingredients for a nice platter of raw vegetables for dipping in a batch of mayoli (see page 60).

Le Grand Mayoli
(Napa Valley Picnic-style)

Some gourmets may be shocked at even the thought of Aioli made with mayonnaise from a jar off the market shelf. Of course we realize that this is not the true and highly esteemed French Aioli. I like to think of it as the next best thing when I'm away from home and traveling without my mortar and pestle.

Let's begin this small sacrilege with shopping for our feast, the object being to assemble the freshest variety of seasonal raw vegetables to dip in the mayoli. A local farmers market is your best bet for Napa-fresh choices that might include:

sprigs of Italian parsley

arugula leaves or watercress, for spice

asparagus

baby carrots

broccoli

button mushrooms

cauliflower

crisp romaine leaves

cucumber

fennel bulb

hulled tender spring fava beans

multicolored radishes

small new potatoes (raw in moderation)

spring onions

sweet peppers

tiny squash

tomatoes

Dress your presentation of washed and prepared vegetables with freshly ground black pepper and maybe some pocketknife shavings of hard cheese, like an aged Sonoma jack or Bellwether pepato. We like to take an accompaniment of cracked crab in season, cold roast chicken, or slices of fully cooked mild sausages. Bon appétit!

■ Sandwich Suggestions

Roughly cut slabs of rustic walnut bread, smeared with rich, soft Camembert cheese, and a couple of slices of fat, ripe tomato. Season with black pepper, and a cornichon on the side. Wash it all down with a good cool local Rosé, perhaps the Vin Gris from Robert Sinskey.

Mild goat cheese on potato bread, Ducktrap pepper-smoked salmon, a few capers and thin shavings of red onion. Great with any Napa sparkling wine.

Split ripe black figs in season, mayoli, mixed lettuce greens, cornichon, and thick-cut honey ham on fresh bakery hamburger buns. Call ahead and arrange a winery tour, then enjoy your sandwiches with a lovely Chardonnay.

Sweet, fully cooked bay shrimp, mayoli, chopped hearts of romaine, and a nice squeeze of lemon on a split soft roll. Spring onion on the side and a cool bottle of Chenin Blanc from the Pope Valley Winery.

Jimtown Store Famous Olive Salad on baguette with a soft, creamy Brie. Just get wine!

◆

The basic drift of this rambling musing on the sandwich is:

- ∽ Choose the bread with your nose.
- ∽ Choose the filling from memory and with your eyes.
- ∽ Follow your heart out into the vineyards.

■ Recipe Tips for Traveling Light

Today's vagabond is a lucky soul, what with fresh, seasonal, local farm produce and all the tasty prepared foods conveniently packaged for travel. He or she will find fully cooked and tasty sausages from Gerhard's Napa Valley Sausage Company, local cheeses from a multitude of makers, and dips and spreads from a wealth of California producers. Combine all this with world-class, fresh-baked breads, and the picnic chef has a full range of shopping choices from which to craft a meal.

Travel light and take advantage of local deli counters. Purchase imported or local cheeses, cured meats and salamis daily by the ounce. Choose the smallest quantities available for the freshest meals.

Sharing picnic meals with fellow travelers is always a fun option. Preparing for four meals is almost as easy as preparing for two. If you find yourself faced with leftover ingredients, the loss can be taken in stride considering the savings of your picnic meals over the price of restaurant dining.

No need to carry briquettes or build an elaborate fire. It takes just minutes to gather twigs and build a tiny fire for toasting bread or grilling those tasty sausages. Any meat or poultry items that are purchased fully cooked can benefit from a pass over the coals to warm and smoke them up. Build a twig fire only where it's allowed and safe. Only use a provided fire ring or barbecue.

Season your meals with lemon, lime, orange or tangerine. They don't take up much room and a good squeeze of lemon can make a world of difference to a store-bought bean or pasta salad.

Talk to the tasting room staff when visiting the wineries, mention your planned meal, and ask for a wine suggestion. Wonderful food and wine pairings can result. Expand on your discoveries in the comfort of your own kitchen. It's a way to take the trip back home with you.

6

Great Picnic Places: Wineries and Roadside Stops

■ Winery Etiquette

We love a wine tour, a day in the countryside, picnicking and a game of bocce. Because this book is basically a picnic guide, we have only listed those wineries that welcome picnickers and that we frequent ourselves. Please don't consider these to be the only places to stop, since the wonderful discoveries you could make in the Napa Valley are simply too numerous to mention.

When visiting, it's good to keep in mind that the winery is an active business on private property. It is a privilege to be allowed the use of their grounds. Often the winery is also the vintner's home, and they're quite literally sharing their back yards with us, so a few customs are worth mentioning:

∽ *Always ask the tasting room staff where to have your picnic.*

∽ *It's appropriate to purchase wine when you plan to picnic on the winery grounds.*

∽ *Only wines purchased at the winery should be consumed with your meal.*

∽ *No grazing in the winery gardens, unless you've been specifically invited to do so.*

∽ *Please keep in mind the winery hours, and clean up your picnic table before closing time.*

∽ *Remember that the winery is like an open-air factory: mind the workers, trucks and forklifts.*

∽ *Watch your children.*

∽ *Enjoy responsibly and have fun!*

■ Motoring in the Napa Valley

Busy does not even begin to describe the Highway 29 corridor in summer, so we would like to share a few tips concerning traffic safety and Napa Valley highway etiquette.

Between Napa and Calistoga, the Valley is served by two main roads that run basically parallel and are about a mile apart. Highway 29 serves the west and most heavily traveled side of the Valley, and the Silverado Trail serves the eastern and quieter side. Between the two run 18 connecting roads and lanes lined up like rungs on a ladder. Take a look at the map in this chapter, and make a rough plan for your day of touring, keeping in mind the best ways to go with the flow of traffic, and not against it.

Savvy local motorists use these connecting roads to avoid having to make left hand turns onto Highway 29 during peak traffic hours. Even though you may be going only a short distance to the left, it's often much easier to turn right and make a left off Highway 29 onto a connecting lane, and go around the block.

■ Picnic Wineries

Key

1. Madonna Estate Vineyards	**13.** Charles Krug Winery
2. Monticello Vineyards	**14.** St. Clements Vineyard
3. Regusci Winery	**15.** Folie a Deux Winery
4. Robert Sinskey Winery	**16.** Casa Nuestra Winery
5. Robert Mondavi	**17.** Cuvaison Winery
6. Rutherford Hill Winery	**18.** Clos Pegase Winery
7. William Harrison Winery	**19.** Zahtila Vineyards
8. Flora Springs Winery	**20.** Summers Winery
9. Rutherford Grove Winery	**21.** Graeser Winery
10. V.Sattui Winery	**22.** Hans Fahden Winery
11. Martini Winery	**23.** Nichelini Winery
12. Prager Winery	**24.** Pope Valley Winery

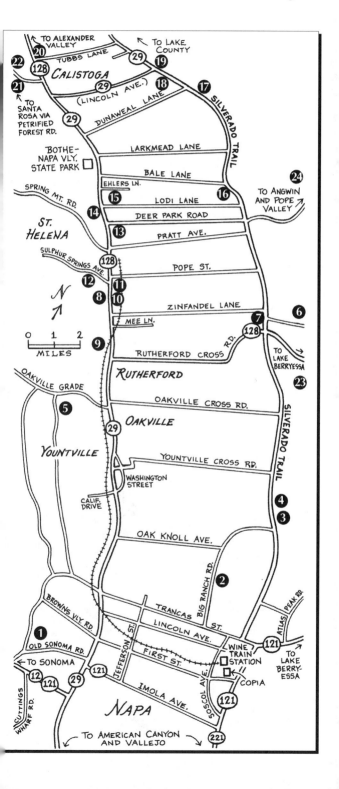

■ Lower Valley

Madonna Estate Vineyards/
Mount St. John Cellars
5400 Old Sonoma Road
Napa 94559
255-8864
Daily 10 a.m. to 5 p.m.

This small, family-run winery is just the sort of place we had in mind when this book was conceived. Third-generation winemaker and vineyardist Andy Bartolucci grows all their grapes in the traditional manner, organically and dry-farmed, adding no extra water besides what nature provides. We believe the old way is the wave of the future and applaud Bartolucci for his commitment to the environment.

They have two picnic areas on site, one always open to the public with tables under vine-shaded arbors, and a second, private one available by reservation only. This beautiful shady nook by a meandering creek is perfect on a hot summer day. Madonna Estate makes all wines in small lots and most are sold at the winery. Besides the Carneros appellation's standards of Chardonnay and Pinot

Bridge on Old Sonoma Road

Noir, they offer three fruity and floral white wines, Riesling, Gewürztraminer and Muscat di Canelli. They also boldly grow a Cabernet on their Carneros estate on a sunny southern exposure that yields an astonishing unique wine.

Monticello Vineyards
4242 Big Ranch Road
Napa 94558
253-2802, 800-743-6668
Daily 10 a.m. to 4:30 p.m.

Since Monticello is not located on either of the two main traffic corridors of Napa Valley, it preserves a bit of that peace and quiet that were commonplace Valley-wide before 1980. Those who have visited the Thomas Jefferson Monticello estate in Charlottesville, Virginia may experience déjà vu since all the buildings, gardens and vineyards are a tribute to his heritage. This well respected family-owned wine house owns five representative vineyards throughout the Valley producing Chardonnay, Pinot Noir, Cabernet, Merlot, Zinfandel, and champagne. Their formal but restful picnic site under olives and sycamores will usually be cool with prevailing breezes blowing north from the bay.

Regusci Winery
5584 Silverado Trail
Napa 94558
254-0403
Daily 10 a.m. to 5 p.m. by appointment only
www.regusciwinery.com

From afar or up close, the light yellow, hand-cut

Regusci Winery

volcanic stone winery is a picturesque old structure. Old pioneer family member T. L. Grigsby built this three-story winery in 1878 using the gravity-flow system of winemaking. By 1932 when Gaetano Regusci became owner, it was a ghost winery. It was resurrected in 1996 by Jim Regusci, where now small lots of Stag's Leap District Cabernet, Merlot, Zinfandel and Chardonnay are made. Two small lawn areas with picnic tables have views that sweep gently down to the Valley floor and the western hills. The Regusci family requests that visits be by appointment only.

Ghost Wineries

The unique setting, soil and climate of the Napa Valley was a big draw to hundreds of immigrant farmers and entrepreneurs in the years following the California Gold Rush. Many of them found the more tranquil work of grape growing and winemaking preferable to the harsh conditions and uncertainties they had encountered in the pursuit of fortune in the gold fields.

The term ghost winery describes the few early Napa wineries remaining that were founded and built between 1860 and the 1890s. Of the dozens of these pioneering vintners in existence in the post-gold boom days, all but a few disappeared due to either vine diseases in the 1890s, economic depression, and/or the bane of Prohibition, in force from 1920 to 1933.

Be sure to ask in the tasting rooms about the fascinating history behind these classic Napa Valley ghost wineries:

Regusci Winery, see previous page.
Charles Krug Winery, see page 79.
Graeser Winery, see page 84.
Nichelini Winery, see page 86.
Pope Valley Winery, see page 87.

■ Mid-Valley

Robert Sinskey Winery
6320 Silverado Trail
Napa 94558
944-9090
www.robertsinskey.com
Daily 10 a.m.to 4:30 p.m.

Pinot Noir is perhaps the most difficult wine to make. As Robert Sinskey has said, it is "the honest wine—it can't hide behind a wall of tannin or a veil of oak." Because Pinot Noir responds poorly to conventional farming, Sinskey has grown it organically since 1991. The result: **Wine and Spirits** *magazine rated their Pinot the number one most requested in our nation's finest restaurants. Take a bottle of their signature wine or Vin Gris de Pinot Noir, a Rosé, out on the terrace of this very new and modern facility. By appointment you can tour the caves and half-acre culinary garden, where culinary director and chef Maria Helm Sinskey grows organic vegetables for special food-and-wine pairing events.*

La Famiglia di Robert Mondavi
1595 Oakville Grade
Oakville 94562
944-2811
Daily 10 a.m. to 4:30 p.m.

The accent on Italian is distinctively pronounced at La Famiglia, strongly reflecting the cultural heritage of Napa's first family. All wines made here are Italian varietals or Italian influenced. Their flagship wine, Colmera, a unique creation of the winemaker, is named for the birthplace of Robert Mondavi's mother Rosa, in the Marche region of Italy.

The spectacular picnic site, in fact the whole winery, is perched on a small, oak- and madrone-

covered knoll on the steep flanks of the western foothills of the Mayacamas. It's a little like visiting a mountainside eyrie. Anywhere from two to a hundred people can enjoy food and wine and play bocce on the small court (with reservations). A popular picnic wine is their Moscato Bianco, a floral, heady Muscat blended with Malvasia Bianca.

La Famiglia is well equipped for special events and by calling ahead, you can be royally treated to a Tuscan-inspired food and wine experience in the Sangiovese Room, on the Balconata, the Terrazzo or in the (bottle) Wine Library.

Rutherford Hill Winery
200 Rutherford Hill Road
Rutherford 94573
963-1871
Daily 10 a.m. to 5:30 p.m.
www.rutherfordhill.com

Rutherford Hill (RH) is one of the Valley's great destinations because it excels in so many areas. First, their wine-aging caves are some of the most extensive in North America, with over a mile of tunnels holding 8,000 barrels of French and American oak. The entrance has a tiered hanging gardens style arbor, and beautiful stone arches frame the massive double oak doors. They offer tours daily.

Second, RH was called "one of the greatest U.S. Merlot producers" by **Wine Enthusiast**. *Over 75 percent of their wine is Merlot, with the balance made up by Cabernet, Chardonnay and Zinfandel port. Third,* **Wine Spectator** *called their tasting room the best in Napa Valley.*

Finally, RH has no less than three picnic sites covering almost an acre. Live Oak Grove has seating for 100 people. The 100-year-old Olive Grove was revived by the late Lila Jaeger, and offers a more intimate picnic experience. The Upper Grove is suitable for large groups and catered events. All sites have great views of the Valley. The only downside might be its popularity. **Sunset** *called RH "one of the best places to picnic in Napa Valley," so you might want to visit during the week or very early on a weekend.*

William Harrison Vineyards & Winery
1443 Silverado Trail
St. Helena 94574
963-8762
Thursday through Sunday 11 a.m. to 5 p.m.

When Mario Perelli-Minetti's family emigrated from Milan, Italy in 1902, they brought an 1860 Grand Box piano with them. The family heirloom can be seen at the far end of the tasting room just waiting for someone to bring it to life. After many years in Delano at A. R. Morro Brandy Distillery, Mario bought this property in 1980 and started growing Cabernet, Cabernet Franc and Chardonnay on this eight-acre estate. Out front you can see what a good choice he made; the ashy colored soil is none other than the famed Rutherford dust. Enjoy a very casual picnic here on the large redwood deck and play some bocce on the court out back. Buona salute!

■ Up-Valley

Flora Springs Winery
Tasting Room: 677 St. Helena Highway
St. Helena 94574
967-8032
Winery: 1978 West Zinfandel Lane
St. Helena 94574
963-5711
Daily 10 a.m. to 5 p.m.
www.florasprings.com

Flora Springs was built two decades ago as a joint venture of the Komes and Garvey families. With Ken Deis as winemaker, all original personnel are still together making fine wine. Their signature wine is appropriately called Trilogy, a traditional Meritage-style wine blending Cabernet Sauvignon, Cabernet Franc and Merlot.

When Sattui's across the highway gets a little crowd crazy, Flora Springs' tasting room is a good, convenient alternative. Inside the spacious new building are a circular bar, wine and picnic accessories and a decent book selection. Outside you'll find the downstairs picnic site of a half dozen tables under young camphor trees and the upstairs option with a small arbor. From upstairs Flora Springs Winery is visible at the foot of the western hills. Customers of 29Joe's coffee shop next-door, another family venture, share the seating.

Rutherford Grove Winery
1673 St. Helena Highway
Rutherford 94573
963-0544
Daily 10 a.m. to 4:30 p.m.
www.rutherfordgrove.com

As a Valley resident, for many years I passed by Rutherford Grove hundreds of times without turning in. What an oversight. This small, family-run establishment has an open, inviting tasting room, excellent wines and a marvelous expanse of lawn surrounded by a 100-year-old grove of red gum (eucalyptus). It's a relatively little known picnic site

Bridge at Zinfandel Lane

considering its prime location off Highway 29.

The modest demeanor of the winery belies its accomplishments. The **Wall Street Journal** *named them one of their five favorite tasting rooms in the Napa Valley. Also the* **Journal** *named their Petite Syrah, sourced solely from the Preston vineyard in St. Helena, one of the ten best wines in California. They're also home to the Napa Valley Grapeseed Oil Company, a natural vegetable oil that is environmentally friendly and good for you.*

Note: The Napa Valley Shakespeare Festival has moved to Old Town Napa (see page132).

V. Sattui Winery
1111 White Lane
St. Helena 94574
963-7774
Daily 9 a.m. to 6 p.m.
www.vsattui.com

Depending on your viewpoint, Sattui is either the Versailles Palace or the Disneyland of Wine-Country picnicking. They have everything: a beautiful, hand-hewn stone winery, sumptuous picnic grounds under 250-year-old oaks, the most-awarded wines in the county, and a deli that is one of the best in northern California. You can buy

Recent Stonework History

The beautiful stonework employed in the construction of the V. Sattui Winery looks for all the world to be straight out of the nineteenth century. Even if you look close at the details, the handwork and the tool marks don't lead one to believe that a building such as this could have been raised up within living memory. The evidence, however, can be deceiving. The old world craftsmanship involved in this building was actually handed down over the years to a couple of contemporary local masons, Danny Scott and Robert Gastelum.

It's a heroic undertaking to build such a structure using traditional methods. The work also took a heroic commitment by Daryl Sattui to honor his grandfather Vittorio, to whom he dedicated the new 18,000 square foot winery upon its completion in 1985, the centennial year of the family business.

ready-made lunches, but with nearly 200 imported and domestic cheeses, meats, homemade salads and desserts, it's much more fun to select a custom meal.

The tasting bar is the longest we saw in our research, and the selection of wines is staggering: over 30 sparkling, white, blush, red, and dessert wines plus Italian varietals grown in Tuscany. Their flagship wine is Preston Cabernet from Rutherford. In fact, fourth-generation winemaker and astute businessman Daryl Sattui has grape contracts with many of the best local growers like Morisoli, Quaglia, Navone and Frediani.

Sattui offers a plethora of wine-related experiences—several private tour and tasting packages, catered group picnics, catered dinners, weddings, and benefits for cellar club members like a private tasting room located in the aging cellars.

If you like company, Sattui is your place, but for a more peaceful experience come off-season during the week.

Martini Winery
254 St. Helena Highway South
St. Helena 94574
963-2736
Daily 10 a.m. to 4:30 p.m.
www.louismartini.com

During the middle of the twentieth century, from the repeal of Prohibition through the 1950s, only a handful of wineries were standard-bearers for the Napa Valley name, and Martini was one. Three generations after Louis M. founded it in 1933, it's still family-run. In 1938 they purchased one of the most celebrated vineyards in the Wine Country, the Monte Rosso. Both their Cabernet and the old-vine Zinfandel (120 years old!) from the Sonoma Valley vineyard should not be missed. A relaxed atmosphere pervades Martini, and the tasting staff is a fun group. (Tip: join the wine club and get a great discount). The picnic site, Martini Park, is practically a secret although only a step off Highway 29 just south of St. Helena. The lawn, shaded by plane trees, has eight tables in the shadow of the historic Boston ivy-covered winery.

Prager Winery and Port Works
1281 Lewelling Lane
St. Helena 94574
963-PORT (7678) or 800-969-PORT
Daily 10:30 a.m. to 4:30 p.m.
www.pragerport.com

As you squeeze down narrow Lewelling Lane to the tiny parking lot behind Sutter Home's Victorian and note the property of only two acres holds a winery, a private residence, gardens and a vineyard, you learn an instant lesson in efficiency. Since 1979 Prager Port Works has been a true family affair, headed by Jim and Immogen and their three sons, two daughters and spouses. Just 3600 cases are made annually of their drier-style red, white and tawny ports plus a Cabernet Sauvignon. Only one or two tables are available for picnicking, so please call ahead. In the spring the gardens hold roses, red poppies, and columbines. A small, entirely appropriate statue of Bacchus greets visitors on the garden path, and so may Use, the winery cat, often seen lolling about or perhaps pining for his friend Less, who is no longer with us.

Charles Krug Winery
2800 Main Street
St. Helena 94574
967-2201
Daily 10 a.m. to 5 p.m.
www.charleskrug.com

It's 1861, Abe Lincoln is president, the American Civil War has just begun, and Charles Krug Winery is founded, the first in Napa Valley. When you walk on the grounds of Krug Winery you touch the very beginnings of what has become the most celebrated wine region in the world (with the possible exception of a few places in France). Owned by the Mondavi family since 1943, Krug is a great place to begin a wine tour, picnic under ancient heritage oak trees, and sip a bit of our own cultural heritage.

Peter Mondavi, Sr., and his two sons, Marc and Peter, Jr., own 800 acres of choice land in the Valley, making Cabernet, Sauvignon Blanc, Pinot Noir, Zinfandel, Merlot and Sangiovese. Check out the way-better than average gift shop with their two tasting bars, chilled white wines and champagne, and a fine selection of books by local authors.

Cabernet harvest

St. Clement Vineyards
2867 St. Helena Highway
St. Helena 94574
800-331-8266
Daily 10 a.m. to 4 p.m., reservations recommended
www.stclement.com

St. Clement is quite simply a beautiful, classy destination. The old Victorian built in 1878 was saved from the wrecking ball in 1962 by Michael Robbins of "Falcon Crest" fame and lovingly restored to its original grandeur. Although recently owned by a series of corporate owners, the small estate charm is intact. From the historic stone-terraced vineyard in front to the front veranda—replete with porch swing—to the flower-bordered walks leading to a century-old olive grove in back, every detail within and without is immaculate. Picnickers can choose from shaded bistro tables and benches in front to a sunny lawn site next to the rose garden. It's best to call in reservations, because St. Clement is very popular.

Folie à Deux Winery
3070 North St. Helena Highway
St. Helena 94574
963-1160, 800-473-4454
Daily 10 a.m. to 5:30 p.m.
www.folieadeux.com

The winery was founded by two psychiatric professionals with a shared dream in 1981. Their friends told them they were suffering classic symptoms of folie à deux, a shared delusion, and the winery's name was born. The tree-lined driveway leading to the bright yellow house on the knoll, so visible from the highway, is a magnet for both tourists and locals. New owners have done a beautiful job restoring this old farmhouse built by a Spanish prizefighter in the late nineteenth century. Take your lunch and a bottle of La Petite Folie Ménage à Trois, a fruity crisp wine the staff calls the ultimate picnic wine, out under great spreading oak trees. Your perch on the knoll as the land sweeps down and away before you is a little like the feeling in a crow's nest. Maybe that's a bit delusional, but not unknown in these parts.

Casa Nuestra Vineyards
3451 Silverado Trail
St. Helena 94574
963-5783
Daily 10 a.m. to 5 p.m.
www.casanuestra.com

Casa Nuestra ("our house") is an appropriate name for this small (3000 cases a year) winery founded by Gene and Cody Kirkham in 1979. It's so much like a private homestead that I felt like a trespasser approaching via the narrow graveled road. The tiny yellow farmhouse/tasting room/office is flanked by an old barn and tractors. In between sits a beautiful grassy picnic site under oak trees. A raised redwood deck thoughtfully built around several valley and black oaks holds a few vintage picnic tables.

The owners' good stewardship toward the land— dubbed the "casa verde" concept—includes recycling, conservation, integrated pest management. and the various use of feathered and furry friends to crop the grasses. Winemaker Shay Boswell makes a dry Chenin Blanc, a Cab Franc, a Meritage and Tinto, a unique field mix. All wines are a great value at $10-$23 a bottle.

Casa Nuestra once had an Elvis sighting—yes, for real. Elvis filmed **Wild in the Country** *here in 1962 and was seen stumbling through a swimming hole of the Napa River. A boulder he rested at briefly was named Elvis Rock.*

Cuvaison Winery
4550 Silverado Trail
Calistoga 94515
942-6266
Daily 10 a.m. to 5 p.m.
www.cuvaison.com

In the early seventies Cuvaison was known for their big, fully extracted red wines when Philip Togni was winemaker. In 1979 they purchased 400 acres in the Carneros for grape land. With John Thacher as winemaker since 1982, their Chardonnays have become known as some of the best in the world. Visiting the winery, it's evident that quality is a part of every aspect of the operation. The tasting room, the offices, and the picnic grounds are all immaculate. They have three picnic sites, the front site under oaks 350 years old. The recent purchase of land on Mount Veeder intended for Cabernet brings them full circle.

Springtime along the Silverado Trail

Clos Pegase Winery
1060 Dunaweal Lane
Calistoga 94515
942-4981
Daily 10:30 a.m. to 5 p.m.
www.clospegase.com

The first time you see it, it's a shock. Looming out of the California pastoral landscape of gray and spring greens, the brightly colored Michael Graves-designed, terra cotta temple to wine and art seems so out of place, like suddenly being teleported to Knossos on the island of Crete. But come to think of it, that was a Mediterranean climate too. It's an enjoyable feeling of dislocation as you tour the grounds featuring works by the world's great modern artists.

The single picnic site has three tiny tables under young walnut trees and a three-foot-high terra cotta ashtray. Inside, the lavish gift shop has a cold case with picnic foods like cheeses, salamis and olives. Every third Saturday is a multimedia event not to be missed titled "A Bacchanalian History of Wine Seen Through 4000 Years of Art."

Zahtila Vineyards
2250 Lake County Highway
Calistoga 94515
942-9251
Daily 10 a.m. to 5 p.m.
www.zahtilavineyards.com
May is the ideal time to visit this up-valley winery when the rose gardens are in full bloom. The two picnic sites are for small and large groups (six or more, please call ahead). Formerly Traulsen Vineyards, young Colorado emigrants John, Sandy, Tony, and Laura Zahtila carry on the tradition of making fine Zinfandel from 60-year-old vines in the Dry Creek appellation of Sonoma County's Alexander Valley. Corey Beck is the winemaker, whom we'll hear a lot more about in the future. The place is bustling with new energy as plans for a new tasting room come to fruition. Just seconds away and adjacent to the two-acre estate Zinfandel vineyard is the trailhead for the Oat Hill Mine Trail. If you're feeling energetic, you'll find plenty of great picnic sites up the five-mile trail.

Summers Winery/Villa Andriana
1171 Tubbs Lane
Calistoga 94515
942-5508
Daily 10 a.m. to 5 p.m., winter 10 a.m. to 4 p.m.
www.sumwines.com
This new facility, opened in 1997, welcomes groups of six or fewer on a drop-in basis. Have friendly and knowledgeable tasting-room manager John Lahey show you the working demonstration vineyard where seven varieties are grown. It's not unheard of for guests to help out with crown suckering in the spring while boning up on vineyard management practices.

Summers is home to the Mount St. Helena Bocce Club and hosts league championship play each year. Visitors will enjoy picnicking under a wisteria arbor, sipping winemaker Corey Beck's award-winning Merlot or Charbono, and rolling a few bocce balls on their regulation-size court, while marveling at the unobstructed views of Napa Valley's grand dame, Mount St. Helena.

Note: Bonsai enthusiasts will like John's Cabernet grapevine on display in the tasting room—five years old, six inches high. Production: one grape bunch each year. Talk about the ultimate stress on a vine—has anyone tried making wine from bonsai?

Graeser Winery
255 Petrified Forest Road
Calistoga 94515
800-898-4682
Daily 10 a.m. to 5 p.m.
www.graeserwinery.com

Picture this: You're sitting at a table under olive trees with a great green expanse of lawn all around you. Behind you are the old yellow farmhouse and outbuildings from 1886. In front your eyes easily clear the incredibly long, low, red chicken coop (mirrored by the red poppies in the garden nearby) to the neat vine rows running steeply from hill bottom to top, and right out to the sky. Framing the hill on either side are giant forest trees, some with limbs big as most trees. You're enjoying perhaps the prettiest picnic site in Napa Valley.

Your host is the hospitable Richard Graeser, who

Graeser Winery

will never charge a fee for tasting and makes every attempt to greet you upon arrival. Formerly a Marine, then an Imperial County farmer, he is making great strides in his third incarnation as winemaker. All wines are grown on the 10-acre estate: Cabernet, Merlot and Cab Franc. Besides the main picnic site there are three others, one a stiff hike uphill to a single table with eye-popping views of the rocky Palisades above Calistoga.

Hans Fahden Winery

Hans Fahden Winery
4855 Petrified Forest Road
Calistoga 94515
942-6760
Weekends 10 a.m. to 2 p.m., weekdays 10 a.m. to 4 p.m.
www.hansfahden.com

Straddling the Mayacamas Mountains above Calistoga, Hans Fahden, in the family since 1909, belongs to both Sonoma and Napa counties. We thought it a unique destination not to be missed. Third-generation Fahdens Antone and Lyall have transformed the old Prohibition-era prune orchards to Cabernet vineyards, their sole wine. The shallow, volcanic soil (only one foot deep—the roots must grow horizontally after striking hardpan!) grows tiny berries of intense flavor and color. Extraction is never a problem; in fact, sometimes they remove the skins before fermentation is over.

A lawyer by training, Antone Fahden has found his passion in gardening and spent the last 22 years developing a landscape inspired by the Monet Gardens outside Paris. There are four rain filled ponds with koi, geese and ducks, water lilies and cattails, all for natural filtration. A tea house, a great picnic site, overlooks the ponds, rose and wisteria arbors, and Japanese lanterns that light the paths at night. Plants are part indigenous and part exotic, like the weeping sequoia that grows a curvilinear trunk.

The picnicker has several choices, including hiking trails that lead to majestic views of Mount St. Helena. By reservation they can offer private weddings (100 per year), corporate conferences, wine cave dinners, and birthday parties. Also it's probably the only winery in the state with guided float-tube fly fishing.

Nichelini Winery
2950 Sage Canyon Road
St. Helena 94574
963-0717 or 800-WE-TASTE (938-2783)
Saturday and Sunday only, summer 10 a.m. to 6 p.m,
winter 10 a.m. to 5 p.m.
www.nicheliniwinery.com

The place to go if you like back country roads, shady picnics, nineteenth-century hand-hewn stone cellars, and real folks with good stories to tell. Four grandchildren of Swiss-Italian immigrant Anton Nichelini, who settled here in 1884, still run this historic winery, making it the oldest family-run winery in Napa County. Practice your bocce technique on their regulation-size court, picnic under 100-year-old walnut trees, or heck, get married there like some friends of ours did and have a big party.

They specialize in reds grown in nearby Chiles

One of the original buildings at Nichelini

Valley, especially old-vine Zinfandel produced from the same vineyard since 1890. They make an unusual white wine too, called Sauvignon Vert (a Muscadelle), made from a 1946 planting. Ask about the Prohibition-era days when winemaking operations were supposed to cease. The Nichelinis had a small "facility" up the hill with a pipe that ran to the main property. With the turn of a lever the pipe would transport either spring water or wine, depending on the proximity of the feds. Turning water to wine was an everyday miracle!

Pope Valley Winery

Pope Valley Winery

6613 Pope Valley Road
Pope Valley 94567
965-1246
Saturday and Sunday 10 a.m. to 4 p.m., weekdays by appointment only (For large groups, always call ahead).
If you want to get away from the glitz and glitter of Napa Valley proper, this true backroads winery is the ticket. The winery was constructed in 1897 by Ed Haus, a Swiss blacksmith, from timbers brought from the nearby Oat Hill Quicksilver Mine. It was built into a hill on three levels using the old gravitational-flow system for processing grapes. The old winery is still used, and several adjoining structures like a blacksmith shop and a wagon shed are intact, too. The new owners are enthusiastic about making fine wine that is value-priced, like their Pope Valley Merlot and Zinfandel and an outstanding Chenin Blanc, all of which have received awards. There are several possible picnic sites around the rustic property.

■ Parks for Picnics

Pioneer Park
On Cedar Street, one block north of Lincoln
Calistoga 94515
942-2838 (City Parks and Recreation)

In summer when the streets of Calistoga are so hot they conspire to make a one-pot mulligan of residents and visitors, head over to the town's main park. Founded in 1936 in honor of Calistoga's pioneers, the park's many sycamores, cedars, redwoods and palms make almost a solid canopy of shade. Many picnic tables are available with barbecue facilities, restrooms, and a great playground for the tykes. Special events are held here annually like Art in the Park and music concerts centered around the gazebo. At the back is a path leading to a low-water crossing of the Napa River where moms watch children wade. The path leads easily to the Sharpsteen Museum, City Hall and the police station on Washington Street. Parking is on Cedar Street and adjacent Spring Street.

Heather Oaks Park
Denise Lane
Calistoga 94515
942-2838 (City Parks and Recreation)

Heather Oaks is a small residential park two miles north of town that gets used by locals 99 percent of the time. It's not for large and/or boisterous groups. There's a large flat lawn space with tables and barbecues under blue oaks. A path leads over a footbridge that spans the confluence of Garnett Creek and the Napa River leading to Mount St. Helena Golf Course.

Robert Louis Stevenson State Park
On Highway 29 eight miles north of Calistoga
942-4575

The great thing about this site is that even though a hundred people could be hiking the Mount St. Helena Trail, the picnic tables are rarely in use. OK, so there's no restroom, the nearest water is two miles north, and not a deli in sight. You didn't come up here for those amenities. You came for the clean mountain air, the big firs, maples and madrones, and to stand in the very footsteps of the famed Scottish author who spent a six-week honeymoon here in the summer of 1880. Stevenson, whose cabin was up the hillside, would pick up his mail and sit on the veranda of the gray two-story house "jammed hard against the hillside." There he enjoyed watching visitors using the croquet ground where today's picnic tables sit. It's likely he took notes here too for his minor classic work, **The Silverado Squatters***, detailing his summer idyll.*

For a little exploring, look for remnants of the Old Toll Road on either side of the grounds. For a lot of exploring, take the summit trail, 10 miles round trip, or the great Palisades Trail (starts across the highway) 11 miles one way to Calistoga. Please bus your table—there's no trash pickup here.

Overshot waterwheel at Bale Grist Mill

Bothe-Napa Valley State Park
3801 North St. Helena Highway
Calistoga 94515
942-4575
www.napanet.net/~bothe
Numerous shady picnic sites, a swimming pool, a year-round stream, superb hiking trails and a recent drop in admission to $2 make Bothe a no-brainer. It's the best. The adjoining Bale Grist Mill is the finest preserved structure of its kind in the country. You can drive to it, or better yet hike the History Trail from Bothe, a short mile-long jaunt through forest and meadow. Visit the native garden next to the Visitor Center where Native American Wappo people still

collect plant materials for ceremony. The Visitor Center, once the home of George Tucker whose father rescued the Donner Party, offers nature exhibits, books and friendly advice. Two popular annual events are Old Mill Days and Pioneer Christmas in the autumn and winter months. Campers have fifty sites to choose from at $12 a night.

Lyman Park
Main Street between Pine and Adams
St. Helena 94574
967-5706 (City Recreation Department)
St. Helena probably has more parks per capita than any town in the county. Downtown Lyman Park, St. Helena's main passive-use park, is meticulously kept. Many tables and barbecues are available and popular with the locals. Great old deodar cedars, oaks and incense cedars shade most of the park, but you can catch a tan on the expansive lawn space. The summer concert series featuring local talent is a well-attended tradition. Other amenities include restrooms, potable water, and small kids' playground, with parking on Main Street or on Railroad Avenue out back.

Crane Park
Valley View Street south of Grayson Avenue
St. Helena 94574
967-5706 (City Recreation Department)
This is St. Helena's largest and only active-use park. Picnic tables are on either a first-come, first-served basis, or groups may reserve deluxe sites with multiple tables, barbecues, and sinks with running water under shady oaks. You'll find lots of lawn too. Family reunions are popular here and recreational choices are many: tennis, volleyball, soccer, a skateboard park, and six bocce courts (evening league play takes precedence). Friday mornings from May to September, the Farmers Market is a true community gathering featuring local and regional organic foods, juices, baked goods, cut flowers, garden plants and accessories, wares by local artisans and live music. It's one of the best ongoing events in town.

Mary Elizabeth Fryer Park
Mitchell Drive and Voorhees Circle
St. Helena 94574
967-5706 (City Recreation Department)
St. Helena's newest neighborhood park is still growing in, so shade is minimal. It has three tables, a kids' playground, and nearby, ducks and geese on the pond. From Sunshine Market, it's two blocks west on Mitchell.

Lewis Station
Corner of Hunt Avenue and St. Helena Church Street
St. Helena 94574
967-5706 (City Recreation Department)
St. Helena's Lilliputian park has three tables under an arbor and flowering pear trees. Past trouble has brought on a no-alcohol-any-time rule.

Stonebridge Park
Corner of Pope Street and Silverado Trail
St. Helena 94574
967-5706 (City Recreation Department)
Created by the town's Beautification Committee in 1982, Stonebridge is picturesquely located beside the Napa River and the Pope Street Bridge, an architectural masterpiece built in 1894. You'll see hawks, herons and other avian life, plus have a great view of the bridge (especially in winter) built by Chinese labor. Despite its age, engineers recently declared the bridge safe to carry the heavy traffic it now bears. There are no facilities besides water, so bring a blanket for the lawn. Park on Pope just west of the park.

Pope Street Bridge

Dry Feet

The first European immigrants to set up shop in the Napa Valley found a place of enormous agricultural potential blessed with a perfect combination of good soil, mild climate, and an amazing supply of fine water courses crisscrossing the landscape. Waterwise, it was a classic good news/bad news situation. On the one hand, you had an elaborate network of year-round and seasonal creeks all making their rambunctious way down to the Napa River. On the other hand, you had all these creeks, gullies, and the winter-rowdy Napa River itself to find your way over, around, or through.

In their characteristic way, the new arrivals wasted no time in making the well-watered landscape fit their own, old-world image of productive and habitable countryside.

The result is a network of dozens of graceful and functional hand-cut stone bridges that have survived from the more than one hundred that were built between 1860 and 1910.

If you find your way to downtown Napa in the neighborhood of Pearl Street where it crosses Main Street, you'll see two fine examples of nineteenth century highway engineering still in use today.

North of Calistoga on Highway 29, one and a half miles north of the Silverado Trail junction, you'll see two fine old stone bridges. There's a place to pull over and enjoy the view out over the flat expanse of Clos Pegase's Palisades Vineyards up to the imposing volcanic heights.

George Yount Park
At Washington, Madison and Jackson Streets
Yountville 94599
944-8712 (Town Recreation Department)
This park and the nearby cemetery are named for Napa's first settler, whose original homestead is commemorated on Yount Mill Road just north of town. Yount Park has a great big old lawn, around which are a dozen tables under redwood trees. You'll find lots of parking on Jackson Street with new restrooms, a kids' playground, and bike racks— handy if you two-wheel in.

Next door is George Yount Pioneer Cemetery and Ancient Indian Burial Ground, established in 1848. Pay respects to other former pillars of the community, like the prolific Grigsby family, as you stroll under big oaks, cedars and camphors. To the north are views of the mostly undeveloped Yountville Hills, the oak and grassland habitat featuring stupendous flower displays in spring, a great example of what the Valley looked like when George first arrived.

Yountville Veteran's Memorial Park
Corner of California Drive and Washington Street
Yountville 94599
944-8712 (Town Recreation Department)
A fairly new linear park, sandwiched between the surface streets and the highway, created for the guys at the Veteran's Home nearby. It's not exactly set up for picnicking, but you might find a couple of benches to relax and have a sandwich. Every Fourth of July they have a celebratory event nearby with fireworks.

Vineyard View Park
Parking/access on Oak Circle
Yountville. 94559
944-8712 (Town Recreation Department)
This small, multi-purpose suburban park has some shade trees plus extensive lawn space and tables for picnicking. Towering over the park's namesake vineyard to the east is Stag's Leap. You can play tennis or shoot hoops while your kids frolic on the playground.

Fuller Park

Off Jefferson Street between Oak and Laurel Streets
Napa 94559
257-9529 (City Parks and Recreation)

Fuller is a classic, turn-of-the-century park that takes up a square city block. John Chalmers was the park architect and first superintendent when it was created in 1926. This is a heavily used but well maintained park, with many mature trees like elms and the exotic Monkey Puzzle. Three picnic areas— appropriately named Cedar, Oak and Sequoia— hold many tables and barbecues. A sight you don't see every day are two groves of tree-like camellias over 20 feet high. In the center of the park is the biggest sandbox in town, which holds a jungle gym for kids to monkey around on while their moms and dads chat and watch from the sidelines. Fuller is a pleasant and unpretentious place to enjoy old-time Napa ambiance without a hint of the modern Wine-Country connotations. In fact this could be Anyplace, USA.

Historic Garnett Creek Bridge, Hwy 29

Grapecrusher Park (Vista Point)

Off Napa Valley Corporate Way
Napa 94558
257-9529 (City Parks and Recreation)

The giant bronze figure of a vintner at his hand-crank press, created by artist Gino Miles, became an instant classic when first unveiled in 1988. On close inspection the statue towers over you at 25 feet high. Notice the amazing detail for such a large work. It was placed strategically on a hill overlooking the Napa River as visitors and returning locals get their first dramatic look at the lower Napa Valley.

The park has only a couple of benches, so for a proper picnic bring a blanket to spread on the lawn area. It's best to choose a day when the winds are calm and weather mild because this site is quite exposed to the elements.

Kennedy Park
On Streblow Drive off Highway 121
Napa 94558
257-9529 (City Parks and Recreation)

Napa's main active-use park gets a lot of it throughout the year, but with lawn space on a galactic scale, you'll find some place to call your own. Boating, fishing, hiking, softball, model airplane flight and golf are just some of the many activities. Three main picnic sites are available with lots of amenities.

Skyline Wilderness Park
Corner of Imola and Fourth Avenues
Napa
252-0481

For just $4 visitors to Skyline have access to over 25 miles of multi-use trail for hikers, mountain bikers, and horseback riders, the most in the county. You'll find scads of picnic sites under oaks and, if you want to set up camp, tent and RV sites. A favorite activity is touring the California Native Plant Garden created by the local chapter of the California Native Plant Society. Say hello to godfather Ralph Ingolls, who's there almost every day. On the trails, lots of deer and birds are visible. Though wild turkeys may waddle through the parking lot or pass by your picnic site, park officials discourage their inclusion on the lunch menu.

Westwood Hills Park
Brown's Valley Road, one mile west of Highway 29
Napa 94558
257-9529 (City Parks and Recreation)

This 110-acre, heavily wooded park has limited but excellent picnic facilities, especially if you're willing to walk a ways. Right off the parking lot are a couple of tables and a drinking fountain. The best site is Oak Knoll, the center of Westwood Hills, just a half-mile walk in. This classic grassy knoll with graceful oaks was once the only portion considered for preservation when a subdivision was nearly built in the 1970s. It can be reached more quickly from Thompson Avenue. A few other table and bench sites are found throughout the park.

Alston Park
Dry Creek Road at Trower Avenue
Napa 94558
257-9529 (City Parks and Recreation)
Alston is the open space counterpoint to Westwood's forested hills. This much-loved park has seen many spirited political battles waged by residents at county supervisors' meetings to keep it from development. From either of the two entrances, Alston's two main picnic sites are both a short walk. On the far north side of the park, primitive sites can be found under oaks by a seasonal stream.

Oak Shores Picnic Area at Lake Berryessa

Oak Shores Picnic Area
Lake Berryessa, about 12 miles east of Rutherford off Highway 128
966-2111 (Bureau of Reclamation)
Lake Berryessa is where middle America goes for recreation. Only ten air miles from Napa Valley, it is a thousand-mile stretch in terms of culture. Here you'll find families barbecuing on a summer weekend, young children with waist floats splashing at the shore, groups of teenagers engaged in mating rituals, and adults enjoying fishing, kayaking, windsurfing, water skiing, and—of course—power boating.

Soon after the lake was formed in 1957, resorts begin leasing land from the government. At first it was on a yearly basis, then long-term. Resorts now occupy a good part of the west shore (the east being private), and free access is found only at Oak Shores and Smittle Creek. Fortunately Oak Shores has a number of separate destinations, each offering something different with a total of more than 100 picnic sites, many with barbecues and shade shelters. Some offer space for large groups and special events, some boat launch access, some sheltered coves for swimming, some privacy.

Sometimes the beer-drinking crowd gets a bit rowdy here at Berryessa, and the county sheriff is called to disperse the inebriated, but if you're caught in this rare event (usually holiday weekends), just consider it all part of the ambiance.

Smittle Creek Picnic Area
Lake Berryessa, about 12 miles east of Rutherford off Highway 128
966-2111 (Bureau of Reclamation)
Smittle Creek is smaller and quieter than Oak Shores (and to the north of it) and appropriate for individuals and small groups. You'll find many tables scattered about the blue-oak forested hillocks with barbecues, a water fountain or two, and restrooms. This is a place for fishermen, hikers, wildlife viewers and bicyclists looking for a quiet lunch spot. From here a lakeside trail ambles 2½ miles to Coyote Knolls at Oak Shores. In spring you'll see wildflowers like Ithuriel's spear among the grasses, and only an occasional Dr. Pepper can or an empty Doritos bag. Just to remind you this is not wilderness, the full-throated masculine roar of a 350-horsepower Mercury boat engine is an ever-present possibility to wake you from any reverie

■ Other Picnic Sites

Picnic at Copia
500 First Street
Napa 94559
259-1600
Open Monday, Wednesday, Thursday 10 a.m. to 5 p.m., Friday through Sunday, 10 a.m. to 9 p.m., May through

September; Thursday through Monday, 10 a.m. to 5 p.m., October through April.

If you're planning a visit to Copia, The American Center for Food, Wine and the Arts (see page __), you might want to plan a delicious picnic interlude. The American Market Cafe, 265-5701, on Copia's grounds offers a lovely selection of fresh seasonal items that you can take out into the gardens or down to the riverside.

Also at Copia, the Wine Spectator Tasting Table, 265-5820, offers an incredible opportunity to experience a world of unique wines by the 2 oz. tasting ($2 to $12) or the 5 oz. glass ($4 to $24).

Copia is a grand, educational and fun place to visit.

Vintage 1870
6525 Washington Street
Yountville 94599
944-2451
Daily 10 a.m. to 5:30 p.m.

The former Groezinger Winery and estate is now a Napa Valley icon for shopping, entertainment and special events with half a million visitors a year. Forty specialty shops, galleries and restaurants dish up an orgy of consumer-related activities for the afflicted. Of prime interest is **Vintage 1870 Wine Cellar**, *the finest in the Valley. The tasting bar is always open. Immaculate picnic grounds with manicured lawn, nine tables and umbrellas are located next to the wine cellar.*

Napa Valley Olive Oil Manufacturing Company
835 Charter Oak Avenue
St. Helena 94574
963-4173
Daily 10 a.m. to 5 p.m.

While much of the Valley has changed in recent years, it's a pleasure to visit the Olive Oil Company, which remains almost identical to when I first saw it 30 years ago. This eastside St. Helena business that fits seamlessly into the neighborhood should probably have historical landmark status. Co-owner families Lucchesi and Particelli have been here for generations, bottling oil on-site. Because local olive groves fell victim to the grapevine, they now seek their olive source from the Central Valley. You can buy oil in quantity to take home as well as cheeses, salamis, and other goodies for a picnic in their olive- and orange-tree-shaded grove with half a dozen tables. This old-fashioned establishment with an old-world feel still does all transactions without a cash register. All wall space is taken up with visitors' business cards but the tradition continues by taping strips together and hanging them from the ceiling.

St. Helena Premium Outlets
St. Helena Highway North, 2 miles from downtown
St. Helena 94574
226-9876
Daily 10 a.m. to 6 p.m.
Shoppers of these fine establishments are welcome to use the picnic facilities. There are a few tables out front and in back a dozen more under blue oaks on a grassy knoll.

Silver Rose Inn Spa and Winery
351 Rosedale Road
Calistoga 94515
942-9581, 800-995-9381
www.silverrose.com
This upscale place is ideal for a special weekend retreat. Spa facilities (only for guests) are state of the art. Inn the Vineyard has deluxe rooms, each with a unique theme. Day visitors are welcome at the tasting room. Limited picnic facilities are available for small groups on the deck overlooking a lake. The superheated thermal waters are piped under the lake and cooled to usable temperatures.

Palisades Market
1506 Lincoln Avenue
Calistoga 94515
942-9549
Thursday through Saturday 7:30 a.m. to 7 p.m., Sunday through Wednesday 7:30 to 6:00
This busy little market has a very popular deli, produce, groceries, beer, wine and picnic supplies. Behind the market is a picnic area with four tables under umbrellas.

Old Faithful Geyser
1299 Tubbs Lane
Calistoga 94515
942-6463
365 days a year, 9 a.m. to 5 p.m.

Only three places in the world have Old-Faithful-type geysers erupting at regular intervals: Yellowstone Park, New Zealand and Napa Valley. Calistoga's geyser spouts on yearly average about every 30 minutes, but in the spring when the aquifer is full, eruptions can occur as often as every five or six minutes. For $6 per person, you can be entertained for a couple of hours here. Picnic tables abound with unobscured views of tri-summitted Mount St. Helena. A geologic study has found that this Old Faithful may help predict earthquakes in California, so bone up on your geoscience knowledge by visiting the exhibits. You'll also find some resident animal oddities called fainting goats. They have a medical condition causing them to keel over when frightened. Just five hundred in the world, they are used by ranchers as decoys in herds of sheep to warn of predators—talk about a lousy job!

Petrified Forest
4100 Petrified Forest Road
Calistoga 94515
942-6667
Open daily except Christmas and New Years Day

Along with the Old Faithful Geyser discussed above, the Petrified Forest harks back to the heyday of the roadside attraction. They're both interesting and authentic relics of nineteenth and twentieth century Americana, where you can also enjoy your picnic.

7

Dining Out

As much fun as picnics can be, some days or nights you just want someone else to cook, serve and clean up. With the remarkable variety of restaurants, cafes and delis in the Napa Valley, you'll find it handy to have some inside information on where you might go out to eat and what to expect. The Valley has become home to some of the finest restaurants in the world over the past twenty years. This is no surprise since the combination of world class wine and the fruits of California's celebrated fields and waters happily all coincide here at the top of San Francisco Bay. We advise calling for reservations, particularly for dinner.

■ Down-Valley

Julia's Kitchen at Copia
500 First Street
Napa 94559
265-5700
Thursday through Monday 11:30 a.m. to 4 p.m.; dinners Friday through Sunday, June through September
An integral part of any visit to Copia is having a meal at Julia's Kitchen, the gourmet restaurant "named for the patron saint of the pantry," Julia Child. Under the direction of Chef Mark Dommen, your light California-French meal is prepared in the impressive open kitchen using the best local and seasonal ingredients, including the produce of Copia's own extensive gardens. Call ahead for reservations and a current schedule of visits by celebrated chefs, teachers and vintners.

Tuscany
1005 First Street (at Main)
Napa 94559
258-1000
Dinners every day but Monday
Authentic northern Italian fare complemented by an extensive wine list of Italian and local wines, plus a full bar.

Uva Trattoria Italiana
1040 Clinton Street
Napa 94559
255-6646
Tuesday to Friday 11:30 a.m. to 10 p.m.
Saturday 5 p.m. to 10 p.m., Sunday 11 a.m. to 9 p.m.
Italian cuisine.

Joy Luck House
1144 Jordan Lane
Napa 94559
224-8788
Lunch and dinner daily
Voted best Asian restaurant in KVYN's **Best of Napa and Sonoma Valleys**. *Mandarin, Hunan and Szechuan cuisine without use of MSG.*

Downtown Joe's Restaurant & Microbrewery
902 Main Street (at Second)
Napa 94558
258-BEER (2337)
Breakfast, lunch and dinner daily, full bar
Fun, frolic and food too, featuring a microbrewery on site. Friday and Saturday nights hop.

Alexis Baking Company & Café
1517 Third Street
Napa 94559
258-1827
6 a.m. to 6 p.m. weekdays, until 3 p.m. weekends
A place to enjoy a coffee, a pastry and a newspaper while the world goes by. Alexis has that European-café ambiance so rare outside of college towns. We highly recommend.

Red Rock Grill
1010 Lincoln Avenue
Napa 94558
226-2633
Lunch and dinner every day
Smarter than the average burgers, fish and chips, and chicken.

Genova Delicatessen and Ravioli Factory
1550 Trancas Street
Napa 94558
253-8686
Open every day for lunch only

Genova is an incredibly popular deli with a nearly cult following of loyal customers. Lines are long at lunch, so when ordering a sandwich be sure to grab your choice of bread roll first from in front of the counter and take a number. Even when busy they'll have your order pronto. Coffee and juice bars complement the full deli of homemade hot and cold favorite Italian dishes. Also, stock up here on Italian

Trancas Bridge

delicacies. Olive oil is a good bargain.

Pearl
1339 Pearl Street
Napa 94559
224-9161
Lunch and dinner Tuesday through Saturday, closed Sunday and Monday
A special treat. For those who remember Brown Street Restaurant, Pearl is the newest incarnation for local owners Nicki and Pete Zeller.

Coles Chop House
1122 Main Street
Napa 94559
Serving dinner every day
Perhaps Napa's greatest new success story, they serve up dinosaurian portions for carnivores.

Zinsvalley Restaurant
3253 Browns Valley Road
Napa 94558
Lunch Wednesday through Saturday, dinner Monday through Saturday, closed Sunday
Great food, service and wine list, with the best selection of Zinfandels anywhere.

Bistro Don Giovanni
4110 St. Helena Highway
Napa 94558
224-3300
Lunch and dinner seven days a week
*Veteran restauranteurs Giovanni and Donna
Scala serve traditional northern Italian cuisine
considered the best in Napa by popular consensus.
Full bar includes 250 wines.*

Red Hen Cantina
5091 St. Helena Highway
Napa 94558
255-8125
*This Napa Valley favorite is well known for fun,
great Mexican food and the best margaritas, by the
glass or pitcher. Choose the outdoor patio in good
weather. From north or south look for the giant white
rooster on the front of Red Hen Antiques next door.*

■ Mid-Valley

Bouchon
6534 Washington Street
Yountville 94599
944-8037
Lunch and dinner every day
*Lively upscale brasserie serving classic bistro
cuisine. Check out the unique French zinc bar, cast in
one piece and ingeniously fitted out with all the
cabinetry, plumbing, refrigeration and glass a
barkeep could ask for. One end of the gleaming zinc
bar is always stocked with heaps of chipped ice
topped with the county's best display of exquisitely
fresh local and imported shellfish. The bar at
Bouchon is a charming mid-valley afternoon stop to
refresh the palate with oysters and bubbly.*

Bistro Jeanty
6510 Washington Street
Yountville 94599
944-0103
Lunch and dinner seven days a week
*Chef/owner Phillippe Jeanty has taken his skills
that made dining at Domaine Chandon such a
sensation and created a country bistro so good that*

the **San Francisco Chronicle** *called them the best
new restaurant in the Bay Area in 1998. Jeanty
along with Bouchon and the French Laundry have
made tiny Yountville one of the finest centers for
French dining in the country. Expect perfectly
prepared, classic French neighborhood fare and
atmosphere at this friendly downtown establishment.
The cool marble bar is a soothing place to visit on a
hot afternoon, perhaps enjoying a pot of rillette with
cornichons and a glass of Rosé. The menu covers a lot
of fondly remembered territory. On my first visit,
voilà, faster than le Concorde, I found my time well
spent here was like "un billette retour pour la
France." Entry and exit visas are not required,
although reservations are recommended for dinner
and peak lunch hours in the high season.*

Piatti
6480 Washington Street
Yountville 94599
944-2070
Open daily for lunch and dinner
*Fine dining in a casual atmosphere with a
friendly staff of waiters. Their wood-fired pizzas,
fresh pastas, and rotisserie roast meats are popular
with locals and visitors alike.*

Pacific Blues Café
6525 Washington Street
Yountville 94599
944-4455
Breakfast, lunch and dinner daily
*Maverick American fare served indoors or outdoors
on their spacious patio. Conveniently located at the
entrance to Vintage 1870.*

Frankie, Johnnie and Luigi Too
6772 Washington Street
Yountville 94599
944-0177
Lunch, dinner, full bar daily
*FJ&L do family style Southern Italian/American
comfort food and pizza at moderate prices in a
homey atmosphere.*

Mustards Grill
7399 St. Helena Highway
Yountville 94599
944-2424
Lunch and dinner daily
This place is never not crowded except when closed. Reservations mandatory. The food is phenomenal, but seating is cheek-by-jowl.

My Serendipitous Discovery of Mustards

I never fail to have fun at Mustards Grill. It has long been a favorite stop in the Valley for the lively atmosphere and great food and beverage. My first visit came many years ago when the place was brand new and the talk of the North Bay. I was visiting my sister who was stationed in the Coast Guard at Alameda. I had made my way by BART and thumb and was lucky enough to have someone drop me off for a memorable lunch. I was on my way to the foot of Mount St. Helena and an evening's crawl through the bars of Calistoga.

I recall a party of four arriving by helicopter, a dramatic entry, to be sure. I did not inquire into the details of these folks' fame or fortune. I do know the scraggly hippie enjoying his first glass of Napa Valley wine had every bit as good a time!

Compadres Mexican Bar and Grill
6539 Washington Street
Yountville 94599
944-2406
Lunch and dinner daily, open 8 a.m. weekends
Popular with the happy-hour crowd, this building was once the home of Gottlieb Groezinger, who owned the winery complex that now houses Vintage 1870.

Rutherford Grill
1180 Rutherford Cross Road
Rutherford 94573
963-1792
Open seven days a week for lunch and dinner
A phenomenon since it opened, the Grill provides a comfortable neighborhood atmosphere, with red leather booths, wood-fired rotisserie inside and a wood-burning fireplace for outdoor night dining.

Try the Caesar or hacked chicken salad, and don't miss the knife and fork baby back barbecue ribs. They pour thirty wines by the glass, and if you bring your own bottle, no corkage fee.

La Toque
1140 Rutherford Cross Road
Rutherford 94573
963-9770
Serving dinner Wednesday through Sunday, closed Monday and Tuesday
Not nearly as famous as the French Laundry (make reservations at least two months in advance) or Auberge du Soleil, La Toque offers one of the great dining experiences in the Napa Valley. Elegant attire requested for the dining room.

■ Up-Valley

Green Valley Café
1310 Main Street
St. Helena 94574
963-7088
Lunch and dinner Tuesday through Saturday, closed Sunday and Monday
We come here week after week for great food at reasonable prices. Even though this Italian trattoria fills with locals for lunch and dinner, it's virtually undiscovered by the media and tourists. Their poached salmon is the standard by which we judge all others.

Tra Vigne Ristorante
1050 Charter Oak Avenue
St. Helena 94574
963-4444
Lunch and dinner daily
Elegant dining, food and service above reproach. Always a great experience.

Terra
1345 Railroad Avenue
St. Helena 94574
963-8931
Dinner Wednesday through Monday, closed Tuesday
Chef Hiro Sone and Lissa Doumani have created the standard for elegance and romantic dining in St. Helena. Full bar.

Gillwood's Café
1313 Main Street
St. Helena 94574
963-1788
Breakfast, lunch, beer & wine, espresso daily
The place for breakfast in town, served from 7 a.m. until 3 p.m.

Taylor's Refresher
933 Main Street
St. Helena 94574
963-3486
The Gott brothers have recently reinvented Taylor's, an institution since 1949, and made it even more popular. The Ahi sandwich is scrumptious if you like it rare. All seating is al fresco. They offer old favorites and add new items to the menu often.

Model Bakery
1357 Main Street
St. Helena 94574
963-8192
Open 7 a.m. to 6 p.m. Tuesday to Saturday, 8 a.m. to 4 p.m. Sunday, closed Monday
You can put together a couple of dishes to make a filling meal here. Enjoy the European café-style ambiance hanging with friends or reading the latest issue of the **North Bay Bohemian**.

Tomatina Pizzeria
1020 Main Street
St. Helena 94574
967-9999
Lunch and dinner daily
Mediterranean cuisine with big-screen TV, billiard table, indoor and outdoor seating.

Wine Spectator Restaurant at Greystone
2555 Main Street
St. Helena 94574
967-1010
Lunch and dinner daily
Developed in 1888 as a cooperative winery, Greystone Cellars was at the time of its construction the largest stone winery building in the world. It's now the home of the Culinary Institute of America's west coast campus, and has gracefully weathered the

Greystone, St Helena

turbulent history of the wine industry, including many years of neglect during Prohibition.

Greystone was designed in a popular nineteenth-century Romanesque style, and is famous for its superbly fitted native tufa stone and an early innovative use of iron-reinforced concrete. We recommend you take the time to visit the CIA at Greystone and plan to have a lunch or dinner at the Wine Spectator Restaurant in the creatively converted north wing of the historic old masterpiece.

A Chef, a Farmer and a Winemaker

A chef, a farmer and a winemaker all quite unexpectedly found themselves standing in line at the gates of Paradise. One after another they introduced themselves, and with a bit of small talk were commenting on the luck of having been transported to the threshold of the Eternal Kingdom, even as they were dismayed at their individual and untimely departures from restaurant, farm and winery.

"We were right in the middle of crush, the fruit was just beautiful, and I was on my way to a great vintage," said the winemaker. "We were working so hard I hardly had time to eat, she continued. "I sure could use a bite!"

The farmer said, "Same here. I planted heavy to heirloom tomatoes and the season was booming. I got so caught up in it all, I haven't had a moment to socialize since spring, and I must admit it's a bit of a relief to have some time to shoot the breeze."

"Ay carumba!" said the chef. "Talk about busy! My boss just opened a second location, the pastry chef is *out pregnant, and Anthony Bourdain stole my sous chef. I could use a drink!"*

Just then, there was a fanfare of trumpets, and the gatekeeper stepped out to announce that today there would be a special offer. Groups or individuals would have their choice of one of three custom-tailored eternities.

The chef, the farmer and the winemaker looked at one another a bit bewildered and decided to stick together.

The gatekeeper then congratulated them on their good fortune and showed them over to a set of three doors.

"Might we just have a bit of a peek inside?" asked the winemaker as they stepped up to door number one.

The gatekeeper said, "Suit yourself," and opened the door a crack. Inside were endless acres of perfectly manicured lawn with people serenely coming and going to the sound of golden harps.

"Oh my," said the farmer. Let's have a look at door number two."

"Oh dear," said the winemaker as she peeked in. "More of the same."

"This is the place!" shouted the chef as he followed his ears through door number three to the bustling sounds of a restaurant in full swing. "It's the Wine Spectator Restaurant at Greystone," he enthused. "Truly, I think we have arrived!"

You may not want to spend all eternity at Greystone, but a visit to the Wine Spectator Restaurant can be a heavenly celebration of California's vineyards, farms and kitchens.

Silverado Brewing Company
3020 North St. Helena Highway
St. Helena 94574
967-9876
Lunch, dinner, full bar daily, live music Friday and
Saturday nights
Brewmeister Ken Mee makes his own liquid ambrosia on the premises. They serve delicious American country food that goes well with a brew, with some dishes even cooked in their beer.

All Seasons Café
1400 Lincoln Avenue
Calistoga 94515
942-6828
Lunch and dinner Thursday through Monday, closed
Tuesday and Wednesday
*Since 1983 All Seasons has brought a touch of
class to the up-valley. Recently chefs Kevin Kathman
and Mark Willard have made it even better. As
summed up by L. Pierce Carson in the* **Napa Valley
Register***, "exquisite cuisine at bistro prices." Their
wine shop on the premises has an enviable reputation.*

Nicola's Deli and Pizzeria
1359 Lincoln Avenue
Calistoga 94515
942-6272
Breakfast, lunch and dinner
*Frequented by locals but spa mellowed visitors
wander in too. Their huge breakfasts are moderately
priced, and lunches feature homemade soups. Ten
beers on tap.*

Bosko's Trattoria
1364 Lincoln Avenue, Calistoga
942-9088
Lunch and dinner daily
*The sawdust on the floor is gone, but everything
else is just as good or better since Bosko's moved to the
south side of Lincoln. Italian cuisine—famous big
servings of fresh pasta and wood-fired pizza.*

Café Sarafornia
1413 Lincoln Avenue
Calistoga 94515
942-0555
Breakfast and lunch daily
*Let-your-hair-down, informal family cafe serving
American food with a touch of southwestern flavor.*
The Best of Napa Valley *magazine rated it best spot
for intelligent conversation, so don't be talkin' trash.*

Wappo Bar and Bistro
1326 Washington Street
Calistoga 94515
942-4712
Lunch and dinner every day but Tuesday

Bring your appetite and a sense of adventure as chef Michelle Mutrux brings global cuisine to your table. In good weather they have outdoor dining under a wonderful wisteria arbor.

Catahoula Restaurant & Saloon

1457 Lincoln Avenue, inside the Mount View Hotel
Calistoga 94515
942-2275
www.catahoularest.com
Dinner nightly 5:30 until 10 p.m. weekdays, until 10:30
Friday and Saturday, full bar

Named for the Louisiana state dog, this is a fun place with fun, delectable food. Chef/owner Jan Birnbaum moved to the Wine Country after building his reputation at some of the best restaurants in both New York and San Francisco. At Catahoula he's done it all his own way, putting out original, Southern-influenced down-home fare bright with blended flavors. From the wood-fired oven in the small dining room come pizzas with toppings unlike any you've likely had before. Likewise the many Southern ingredients typically on the weekly changing menu are prepared differently than they are by most chefs. They make their own scrumptious sausages and cured meats, using those in creative ways as well. Birnbaum's unique mouth-watering desserts are worth a visit by themselves. [BL]

Triple S Ranch

4600 Mountain Home Ranch Road
Calistoga 94515
942-6730
Serving dinner, closed January through March

This working ranch is a real throwback to the past. Triple S has traditional cowboy fare like steaks and mashed potatoes, a mountain lodge atmosphere, and moderate prices. Some of the old-timer bar patrons look like they don't get out to anywhere else.

8

Activities and Diversions

■ Food and Wine Education

Any visit to northern California's Wine Country provides an education for the senses. Visitors find a little something new about each year in a place where the people, the seasons, and the soil are so entwined. Our constantly evolving marketplace also ensures that any tasting along the wine roads, a visit to the farmers market, or dining experience will delight you with a new appreciation for the flavors of life.

The lovely valley of the Napa River is particularly well situated for enriching one's epicurean education with its ideal Mediterranean climate, renowned wines and tradition as a place of old world culture on a distinctly American frontier.

Copia
American Center for Food, Wine and the Arts
On the oxbow of the Napa River
500 First Street
Napa 94559
259-1600 for Tickets and General Information
265-5700 Julia's Kitchen
265-5800 Cornucopia Gift Shop
265-5900 Administration
www.copia.org

Copia is a unique place, a place of shared vision and commitment to a centuries-old connection between the quality of life, renewal, and the fertility of the earth. It's a daily celebration of the senses of sight, sound, smell, taste and touch. Copia is a remarkable cultural resource raised up to provide a place of respite, refreshment and education on a lovely setting only a few blocks from downtown Napa.

To try to describe everything that goes on at Copia would not be possible in this guidebook. What we'd like to focus on here is the fantastic educational offerings—free with price of admission—that include daily lectures, demonstrations and tastings, a fantastic library, fully connected computer stations, and the company of a roving troop of informative docents. You may also enroll in a constantly evolving series of workshops, public forums and special lectures, as well as agriculture, cooking and wine classes. Really, it goes on and on, and the place is truly dedicated to enlightenment and education in a highly entertaining way!

Please call or visit online for current schedules of events. See page 101 for more information on Julia's Kitchen. See page 97 for more information on Copia as a premier picnic place!

Culinary Institute of America at Greystone
2555 Main Street
St. Helena 94574
967-1100
www.ciachef.edu
Located in the historic Greystone Cellars building, the CIA offers continuing education and career development classes for food and wine professionals in high-focused formats, as well as an ongoing series of less formal cooking demonstrations for the general public.

Please call or visit online for current class and demonstration schedules. Guided tours of the building and teaching facilities are available to the public Monday through Friday at 10:30 a.m., 1:30 p.m. and 3:30 p.m. for a fee of $3.00. The public is always welcome to visit the Campus Store (see page 29) or the Wine Spectator Restaurant (see page 108).

Goosecross Cellars
Yountville
800-276-9210
Every Saturday at 11 a.m. this little winery offers a free wine seminar course called Wine Basics. Everyone from the novice to the enophile will enjoy it and learn something new.

Old olive grove at St. Clement Vineyards

■ Napa Valley Arts

Mumm Napa Valley Photography Exhibitions
8445 Silverado Trail
Napa 94558
800-686-6272
Mumm presents world-class photography exhibitions that change approximately every two months. Previous exhibits have included Galen Rowell's Bay Area Wild, a fifty-year retrospective of world press photos, and silent film star Harold Lloyd's Rogue's Gallery. Annually they present exhibits showing the best of the Napa Valley Mustard Festival and the Ansel Adams Gallery.

Clos Pegase Multimedia Presentation
"A Bacchanalian History of Wine Seen Through 4000 Years of Art"
1060 Dunaweal Lane
Calistoga 94515
942-4981, ext. 200
On the third Saturday of every month, proprietor Jan Shrem presents a Bacchanalian History of Wine at 2 p.m. With over 100 images from artists like Rembrandt, da Vinci, Chagall and Picasso. Reservations requested.

Di Rosa Art and Nature Preserve
5200 Carneros Highway 121
Napa 94559
226-5991
www.dirosapreserve.com

More than 2000 works of art by contemporary Bay Area artists in a superb rural setting. You must call for reservations before visiting.

Napa Valley Museum
55 Presidents Circle
Yountville 94599
944-0500
www.napavalleymuseum.org
Daily except Tuesday 10.a.m. to 5.p.m.

This modern facility is dedicated to promoting the cultural and environmental heritage of the Napa Valley. Their special changing exhibits represent a diverse range of subjects from fine arts to history to the natural sciences. Their permanent interactive wine exhibit, **California Wine: The Science of an Art***, takes visitors through a year in the winemaking process.*

Sharpsteen Museum and Sam Brannan Cottage
1311 Washington Street
Calistoga 94515
942-5911
Daily noon until 4 p.m.

Founded by Ben Sharpsteen, one of Walt Disney's chief animators, it features fine exhibitions of Calistoga's past.

Ca'Toga Galleria D'Arte
1206 Cedar Street
Calistoga 94515
942-3900

Even people who are not art buffs will enjoy this. Founded by internationally known Italian artist Carlo Marchiori whose home, Villa Ca'Toga in Calistoga, is a monument to trompe l'oeil. Open to the public by appointment, Saturdays only, May through October.

■ Other Views of the Napa Valley

Napa Valley Wine Train
1275 McKinstry Street
Napa 94559
253-2111 or 800-427-4124

Year-round gourmet lunch and dinner excursions on a train pulling luxurious Pullman cars up the

Valley. *Special events include Sunday Jazz Concerts, Family Fun Night, Santa Claus Train, Halloween Ghost Train, Oktoberfest, and Murder Mystery Dinner Theatre.*

Wine Plane
Box 4074
Napa 94559
888-779-6600
Sip wine, enjoy music, and view the Wine Country from a thousand feet up. The wine plane is actually one of two high wing Cessnas, affording unobstructed views. They carry from three to five passengers on flights lasting thirty to seventy-five minutes, ranging as far as the coast.

Sonoma Cattle Company & Napa Valley Trail Rides
P.O. Box 877
Glen Ellen 95442
996-8566
Enjoy the old time tradition of horseback riding in Bothe-Napa Valley State Park. They offer box lunch and barbecue dinner rides, as well as sunset and full-moon specials, plus private parties and corporate retreats.

Modern Southern Crossing Bridge

Hood Mountain Adventures
824-0543
www.hoodmountainadventures.com
The people to call for naturalist-led hikes, rock climbing, and other local adventures.

Hot Air Balloon Excursions

Certainly drifting about high over the vineyards in a basket suspended from a hot air balloon gives you an exhilarating other view of the Napa Valley. Any one of sixteen different companies would be happy to take you up, up and away. Most will also arrange to have a lovely picnic available as well. Please refer to the Yellow Pages under Balloons—Manned *for a complete listing of companies.*

■ Hiking in the Napa Valley

Napa is not as well known for outdoor recreation as neighboring counties like Sonoma and Marin, but once you look past the incredible wine-tasting opportunities, you'll find our Valley is an excellent

Old wall in Knights Valley

venue for bicycling, hiking, and even rock climbing. Spring and fall are the best seasons while winter offers many beautiful days between storms. Summer is often too hot.

The following hikes are recommended for spring or autumn:

The newly opened **Palisades Trail** offers the most exciting hike in the county. To reach it, start at the summit of Highway 29 in **Robert Louis Stevenson State Park** and head east on the **Table Rock Trail** for two miles. From there it hugs the base of the volcanic Palisades escarpment for five miles. Another five miles leads down the historic **Oat Hill Mine Trail** to Calistoga. Car shuttling is your best bet.

The **Mount St. Helena Trail**, also starting at the Highway 29 summit in R.L. Stevenson State Park, is a ten-mile round-trip ascent to the 4,339-foot summit, giving a commanding view of the North Bay. On super clear days in winter the Farallon Islands, the Sierra Nevada, Mount Lassen and Mount Shasta are visible. Winter also gives you a chance to snowshoe once or twice a season.

Skyline Wilderness Park in south Napa offers hiking, mountain biking and horseback riding through a beautiful wooded valley and over high, oak-wooded hilltops.

Recommended for summer hiking:

Bothe-Napa Valley State Park is a heavily forested west side retreat with a year-round stream and redwood groves that stays cool on hot summer days. Lots of historic structures are preserved here including the oldest in Napa Valley, the Bale Grist Mill.

Recommended for winter hiking:

The newly opened **Rooster's Ridge Trail** is a short, one-mile hike, starting just south of Rector Dam in Yountville. You'll find great views of Napa Valley, Rector Reservoir and Haystack Peak.

Winter is the ideal time to visit **Lake Hennesse**y, where dozens of species of birds hang out, including bald eagles and osprey, just a few miles east of St. Helena on Conn Valley Road. There are trails on either side of the lake.

Consider taking your picnic lunch or dinner on a short walk in the hills or a mountaintop sunset hike. You'll improve your appetite, and get away from the crowds too. Picnic totes can be as simple as a handbag to fancy models that come with wine glasses, cutting board, corkscrew and other necessary accoutrements. They are available at local picnic suppliers. If you want more hiking ideas, check a local bookstore for *Great Day Hikes in & around Napa Valley* by Ken Stanton.

■ Rock Climbing in the Napa Valley

Rock climbing in Napa is centered around Mount St. Helena, where climbers in the know can find high quality "pocket" face climbing on volcanic rock that is generally good to excellent. Outside of the main climbing areas, rock quality can vary considerably. All four major sites are either on or close to the main trail or fire road.

The Silverado Mine is a ¾-mile hike just uphill from the Stevenson Monument. You'll find mostly moderate routes on potentially unstable rock.

The Bubble is the most popular site on the mountain, 1.3 miles from the trailhead on the summit fire road. Moderate to difficult routes on good rock are mostly top-roped, but recent bolting allows some leading.

The Bear (aka **The High Rocks**) has some moderate routes but is known for difficult to severe sport climbing routes on steel-hard quartz-like rock. It's found a short distance beyond the Bubble and up a steep hillside. The original Bear route is one of the few long-crack climbs on the mountain whose rough rock and overhanging nature belies its 5.9 rating.

The Far Side was developed as a challenging lead climbing area with over forty moderate to difficult, mostly face-climbing routes. Find a good use trail just left of **The Bubble** and take it fifteen minutes to the ridgeline. Most routes here and at the other sites are less than 75 feet high.

■ Napa Valley Wild

While not much is heard about land in Napa County without a wine-grape connection, much wild land remains by design or chance. One of the first to envision saving land in its natural state was Mollie Patten, tollkeeper on the Old Lawley Toll Road on Mount St. Helena. Long after her death, Robert Louis Stevenson State Park became reality in 1949, when the first 500 acres of forest surrounding the RLS memorial were dedicated. RLS State Park now encompasses well over 4,000 acres.

In 1960 California State Parks bought Reinhold Bothe's Paradise Park to preserve the beautiful Ritchey Canyon, with its year-round stream and redwoods. Bothe-Napa Valley is a well-administered state park with hiking, horseback riding and camping opportunities, and an excellent place to learn about the native Wappo people and the pioneers.

Si and June Foote founded the Napa County Land Trust in 1976. Since then it has saved more than 25,000 acres of wild and agricultural land, becoming one of the great success stories in California. They often work in conjunction with the State Parks Department and other agencies to save the finest examples of Napa's wild lands. These parcels are privately held by individuals who continue to live on their land but who give up certain development rights in exchange for tax benefits and the satisfaction of knowing their land is protected in perpetuity.

Some of these prize parcels include the finest stand of redwoods left in Napa County, spectacular waterfalls, pristine watersheds, and lofty volcanic palisades. The public can access these wonders usually once or twice a year by joining guided hikes conducted by the Land Trust of Napa County, as they are now known. Better yet, help preserve our natural heritage by becoming a member. Contact them at The Land Trust of Napa County, 1040 Main Street, Suite 203, Napa 94559, or call 252-3270.

Other agencies are also active in our county to preserve land. California Department of Fish and Game manages the Napa River Ecological Reserve in

Yountville and Rooster's Ridge Trail east of there. Bureau of Land Management is actively building trails in the Lake Berryessa region. Skyline Park Association is a private organization managing a beautiful watershed in eastern Napa hills where hiking, horseback riding and mountain biking are popular.

There's a strong feeling in our community that not all the hills should be planted to grapes, that what makes our valley special is the backdrop of firs, pines and oaks enclosing these prize vineyards providing beauty, animal habitat, natural erosion control, protection for the Napa Valley aquifer, and an indefinable something else that enriches our lives without measure.

■ Some Other Roadside Attractions

Petrified Forest
4100 Petrified Forest Road
Calistoga 94515
942-6667
Open every day but Christmas and New Year's Day
Stretch your legs on a mile-long trail past three-million-year-old stone redwoods and pines. Paying customers can enjoy exclusive use of the picnic tables near the parking lot.

Safari West Wildlife Preserve
3115 Porter Creek Road
Santa Rosa 95404
579-2551
www.safariwest.com
If you ever wanted to go on an African safari but didn't care for the travel expense and painful cholera shots, this is your place. Four hundred beautiful acres support 350 exotic, endangered and extinct-in-the-wild African mammals and birds. Separately enclosed are the predators: two young cheetahs and a serval cat. See familiar animals like giraffe and zebra and some you've never heard of like addax, lechwe, kob, sitatunga and scimitar-horned oryx. Call to arrange a tour or to overnight in a cozy tent cabin or cottage.

Smith's Mount St. Helena Trout Farm & Hatchery
18401 Ida Clayton Road
Calistoga 94515
987-3651
Weekends February through October
A great place to take the kids. You'll find lots of picnic space here. The Smith family has been here since 1898.

Napa Valley Grapevine Wreath Company
8901 Conn Creek Road (Highway 128)
Rutherford 94573
963-8893
Every day but Tuesday
Founded by Sally Wood whose family has been farming here for three generations. She and her staff create a variety of products like baskets, Christmas trees, lamp shades, hearts, stars and special orders.

■ Taking the Waters

Historic Health Retreats in the Napa Valley

At the foot of our venerable old Mount St. Helena, the earth is still restless. The top of the Napa Valley and the town of Calistoga sit close above its molten past. As long as there have been people around these parts, perhaps some eight or ten thousand years, this Valley and its steaming springs of clear mineral water have been a place of healing and rejuvenation for the body and the spirit. We follow a path well-worn by the feet of the Wappo ancestors to this place held sacred for its dramatic union of earth's fire and pure water.

Indian Springs Resort & Spa
1712 Lincoln Avenue
Calistoga 94515
942-4913
www.indianspringscalistoga.com
Since 1871 the spa at the ancient steam lodge and bathing site the Wappo people called "the oven place" has offered mud baths, mineral tubs, pools and steam rooms. They have cozy bungalows and a beautifully restored 1913 bathhouse, a fantastic Olympic-size thermal pool, a full range of spa

Old church at Calistoga

services, plus lovely grounds and views to the mountains surrounding the Valley.

Of special interest is the fact that the locally owned Palisades Market prepares delicious food and will be happy to deliver it right to your room. I recommend you stop in the market after you get settled into your accommodations. It's located two blocks south of Indian Springs at 1506 Lincoln Avenue, phone 942-9549. They have a great friendly kitchen staff, and there's always something new and delicious being prepared fresh for your picnic or evening's repast. The beauty of the Indian Springs/Palisades Market synthesis is this: You needn't bother dressing in anything more than your robe or pajamas to enjoy an intimate meal with your sweetheart following an afternoon of soaking your bones and reveling in spa services.

White Sulphur Springs Resort and Spa
3100 White Sulphur Springs Road
St. Helena 94574
963-8588
www.whitesulphursprings.com

*A short, pleasant drive west of downtown St.
Helena on Spring Street will lead you up a lovely
stream to the enchanting grounds of White Sulphur
Springs. This historic resort was established in 1852
as a tranquil retreat and remains so to this day. It's
so peaceful, snug at the foot of the mountains with
the sound of falling water and songbird chatter.*

*Lodging options include European-style cozy
rooms with shared baths in the Carriage House, a
rustic inn with fifteen private rooms and three
simple cottages. There's a free-flowing warm
mineral pool beside a waterfall as well as an outdoor
Jacuzzi and large swimming pool.*

White Sulphur Springs Resort History

It's hard to imagine, as you wander the tranquil and
inspiring grounds of this low key and relaxed resort,
so much relatively recent history associated with the
place. Between 1852 and the present numerous
grand hotels, dance halls, cottage hotels and even a
honky-tonk occupied the shaded canyon of White
Sulphur Creek. Over the years each was a brief
success and each in succession fell victim to
disastrous fires.

Around the turn of the twentieth century and at its
prime, the hotel and cottage complex owned by John
Standford offered various accommodations for up to
1000 guests. At one time even a bowling alley was up
there in the canyon full of wildflowers and mighty
redwood trees. The diligent explorer can discover
traces of these past splendors, but most visitors will be
more than delighted to find a forgiving and
encroaching forest quietly burying vestiges of this
roaring past.

■ In Touch: Spa and Massage

<u>NAPA</u>

Somatics Acubodycare
925 Golden Gate Drive
Napa 94558
255-2473
I can personally vouch for the effectiveness of this alternative mind-body approach.

<u>YOUNTVILLE</u>

Veranda Club Spa
6795 Washington Street
Yountville 94599
944-1906

<u>ST. HELENA</u>

White Sulphur Springs Resort and Spa
3100 White Sulphur Springs Road
St. Helena 94574
963-8588
Superb rural setting at the oldest resort in California.

St. Helena Hospital Massage Therapy
650 Sanitarium Road
Deer Park 94576
963-6250

<u>CALISTOGA</u>

The Body Works
805 Washington Street
Calistoga 94515
942-6316
They recently celebrated their 20th anniversary.

Golden Haven Spa Hot Springs Resort
1713 Lake Street
Calistoga 94515
942-6793
Olympic-size heated indoor swimming pool, hot tub and lodging. Couples can get massages in the same room here.

Indian Springs
1712 Lincoln Avenue

Calistoga 94515
942-4913
Olympic-size heated outdoor pool, lodging, spa treatments.

Calistoga Spa Hot Springs
1006 Washington Street
Calistoga 94515
942-6269
Four hot, warm and cool pools, exercise room, spa treatments and massage, lodgings with kitchenettes.

■ Bookstores

Calistoga Bookstore
1343 Lincoln Avenue
Calistoga 94515
942-4123
Fine, independent full-service bookstore run by Reese and Jeanie Baswell. Come in and browse the latest novels, California travel guides, alternative health, local authors, books about Napa Valley, writer's inspirational books. Big, soft couches in back for extended study.

Copperfield's
1330 Lincoln Avenue
Calistoga 94515
942-1616
Newest branch in this small chain offers music, new and used books and a relaxing, browsing atmosphere.

Main Street Books
1315 Main Street
St. Helena 94574
963-1338
California's smallest used bookstore, only 200 square feet. Proprietress Liza Russ has a fanatically faithful following. A small selection of new books.

Pacific Union College Bookstore
100 Howell Mountain Road North
Angwin 94508
965-6271
Mainly textbooks plus a variety of other books for sale. Great selection of office supplies.

Adventist Book Center
19 Angwin Plaza
Angwin 94508
965-7292
Christian books and music.

Bookends
1014 Coombs Street
Napa 94559
254-7323
Often voted Napa's best bookstore in the annual **Best of Napa Valley**. *Great selection of everything plus calendars, magazines, topo maps and reading accessories.*

Copperfield's
1303 First Street
Napa 94559
252-8002
Many new and used books with an awesome variety of alternative-type magazines. Their sale book section is also impressive.

Learning Faire
964 Pearl Street
Napa 9455
253-1024
Children's books, workbooks and toys.

Bookaneer
Napa
259-1578
Out-of-print and antiquarian book search service. By appointment only.

■ Calendar of Events

Please call for dates and details.

JANUARY

A year in the Wine Country starts with a lush green sheen of new grass and a carpet of mustard flowers capturing the eye from the windblown Carneros in the south to the forested slopes of Mount St. Helena. Winery workers are out pruning the vines. New Year is a time of refreshing rains with an occasional warm evening that brings out thousands of frogs in the lowlands, all a-peeping for love.

Napa Valley Mustard Festival
259-9020

This multi-event extravaganza spreads over two months. Among the main events are Mustard Magic, an Awards dinner, the Marketplace with cooking demos, arts and crafts and music, and the Grand Finale photo contest—a black tie dinner at Mumm Cuvee—plus much more.

Different Strokes

The crows in winter share space with the seagulls. The seagulls are in from the coast, sheltering from winter storms. They both eat bugs in the grass out in the ball field. They both scavenge bits and nibbles from the grocery store parking lot.

The crows, however, fly into the trees over the road and drop walnuts onto the pavement, then spend hours picking the tasty nutmeats from the broken shells. The seagulls, I suspect, think the crows quite odd.

Bridge at Highway 128

FEBRUARY

Even though it may still be officially the dead of winter, the daffodils and acacia are whispering "springtime." Pruning continues.

Napa Valley Mustard Festival
259-9020

MARCH

The vines awaken as the previous year's vintage rests quietly in the cellars.

Napa Valley Mustard Festival
259-9020

Napa Valley Marathon
255-2609
One of the prettiest courses in the world attracts both local runners and national talent.

Sun and Stars
963-1614
This benefit for the Montessori Family Center in St. Helena features rare Napa Valley vintages and unique excursion packages in both live and silent auction lots.

APRIL

You'll see the field crews out planting rootstock in newly cultivated fields while the wild iris and lupine riot in the wild places.

April in Carneros
800-825-9475
A chance to visit small wineries otherwise closed to the public as well as larger ones, all offering rare and newly released wines.

Kitchen in the Vineyards Tours
800-965-4827
View five spectacular kitchens, dining rooms, entertainment areas and gardens in the heart of the Wine Country. All proceeds benefit the Napa Valley Chamber Music Festival.

Napa County Iris Gardens: A special place in the spring
9087 Steere Canyon Road
255-7880
During April and May, Lesley and John Painter welcome the public to their unique farm set in the lovely countryside along the road to Lake Berryessa.

The gardens are about a mile and a half north of Highway 128. It's essential that you call ahead for directions and to inquire about the hours of operation and status of the bloom. When you arrive, pick up a list of varieties so you can order the rhizomes of your favorites. You might want to pack a picnic as the Painters provide several tables where you can enjoy your lunch while you plan your own iris planting.

MAY

There's so much new growth in the vineyards that the field crews are all busy training the strong, green canes to the wires of their trellising systems.

Napa-Solano Home and Garden Show
Napa Expo
Four hundred exhibits and hundreds of professionals explain the latest ideas and technology in home improvement, outdoor living, gardening and landscaping.

Sprint Car Races
Napa County Fairgrounds
Memorial Day Weekend

942-5111
The kickoff for an exciting summer of racing.

Calistoga Wineries Annual Open House
942-4437, 888-224-5879
Eight small wineries within minutes of each other offer free wine tasting, food, entertainment and more.

JUNE

Summer comes to call with long, warm days and a strong bloom of roses.

Napa Valley Wine Auction
Meadowood Resort
963-3388, 800-982-1371, ext. 4
The Grande Dame of wine auctions—bring your pearls and your pocketbook.

Art in the Park
Pioneer Park
Calistoga
942-4769
About forty Napa Valley artists exhibit their work, with live music, silent auction, food and wine, and a coffee bar. Benefits the Calistoga Music and Arts boosters.

JULY

July is custom-made for picnics. It's also a time to make reservations for dinner and spend your day at a well-shaded table or patio as you enjoy cool wine and simple salads and sandwiches.

Another Rockin' Fourth of July
Veteran's Park
Yountville
257-9529
Free outdoor party for the whole family. Fireworks at 9:30 p.m.

Napa County Fair
Napa County Fairgrounds
Calistoga
942-5111
Old fashioned country fair with amusement rides,

livestock showings, local art and culinary exhibits, and live country and rock music.

Seminary Street Bridge, Napa

July 4th Silverado Parade
Calistoga
942-6333
Classic small town parade.

Napa Valley Shakespeare Festival
Riverbend Performance Plaza (at the Napa Mill)
500 Main Street
Old Town Napa
251 - WILL
Like Shakespeare's Globe Theatre of old, located on the River Thames in London, the new venue for the Napa Valley Shakespeare Festival is found on the banks of the River Napa, surrounded by the Hatt Marketplace and the Napa River Inn. Seating is still al fresco with your choice of low-back or standard chairs, or chairs with tables. You can make an elegant evening of it, dining at one of many fine restaurants within walking distance of the Plaza.

Wine Country Film Festival
996-2536
Films of social conscience from the world cinema, shown in both indoor and outdoor venues from Sonoma to Napa County. Special tributes have been given for Kirk Douglas, Rita Moreno, Richard Harris, Ernest Borgnine and others.

Summer Concert Series
Mondavi Winery
888-769-5299
Begun in 1969, this is the premier summer event in the Valley. Get tickets early and see the likes of Boz Scaggs.

Summer Concert Series
Lyman Park
St. Helena
963-4456
Good local talent entertains as St. Helena lets down its hair and dances.

Napa Valley Writer's Conference
Napa Valley College
Napa
967-2900
Nationally acclaimed confab for fiction writers and poets. Well known writers give evening readings at wineries around the Valley.

AUGUST

August begins with the cellar crews preparing to receive the coming vintage. Last year's grapes are making their way to the bottling lines, and the Valley's abuzz with anticipation for the coming crush.

Napa Town and Country Fair
Napa Expo
253-4900
This is the real deal, with locals competing for prizes in foods, wines, arts, crafts and 4-H livestock, plus live music, a rodeo and a Destruction Derby.

Wine Country Film Festival
996-2536
See July.

Music in the Vineyards Festival
578-5656, 800-965-4827
Classical music performed by musicians from across North America and Europe at marvelous winery settings.

SEPTEMBER

It's Harvest Time! Everyone is on the run from late August to early October. September is perhaps the most exciting time of the year, and the vineyards simply glow as the leaves begin to take on their autumn color surrounded by the golden hills.

Concert on the River
Downtown Napa
257-0322
The Napa Valley Symphony plays under the stars on Labor Day Weekend.

Calistoga Beer and Sausage Festival & Chili Cook-Off
Fairgrounds
942-6333
Huge crowds try to devour miles of sausages and empty dozens of kegs of microbrews.

Old Stones by Bale Mill

OCTOBER

As the first winter storms sweep majestically in off the Pacific, the grapevines provide a final burst of breathtaking golden and red hues, then loosen their summer-firm grip on their foliage. The rain is a welcome refreshment, and the roses respond with a lovely late season show of color.

Old Mill Days
Bale Grist Mill State Historic Park
963-2236
Music, traditional crafts, period costumes, food and fun.

Hometown Harvest Festival
St. Helena
963-5706
Great arts and crafts, a 5K and 10K fun run and walk, and your household pets en regalia in the Napa Valley's one and only pet parade.

NOVEMBER

The olive harvest begins in the season of Thanksgiving. As the vines begin their winter sleep, the new wines are being carefully tended by the cellar crews who are shepherding them from tank to barrel, while we celebrate the process by raising a glass.

Yountville Festival of Lights
944-0904
All day Holiday Faire kicks off a month-long celebration highlighted by the annual Napa Valley Ice Art Championships.

Carols in the Caves
224-4222
Improvisator David Auerbach, master of more than fifty rare and ancient musical instruments, gives unique performances in winery caves and natural caverns around the Valley.

Napa Valley Viticultural Fair
944-8311
This trade tech heaven takes place every other year at Napa Expo. Napa Valley Grape Growers bring more than 100 vendors, plus educational seminars, hot lunch and wine tasting.

DECEMBER

Olive harvest continues. The grapevines sleep while the field crews prune away the summer's canes. After the excitement of summer and harvest, it's easy to focus one's attention on the particular pleasures of California's wonderfully diverse wine regions. Winter is just a brief interlude of refreshing Pacific storms and a favorite, quieter time to explore the Wine Country.

A Calistoga Holiday Picnic Tale

Often, even in the heart of winter, a fantastic clear day will coincide with a day off, a night away from home, and the truck packed with a basket full of picnic fixings.

On the cusp of the old millennium Jannette and I made reservations to spend a night at the Calistoga Inn, a simple and historic hotel with eighteen rooms, a nice restaurant, and one small award-winning brewery (see page 110).

Christmas Day is a uniquely wonderful and quiet time to enjoy the Wine Country without all the bustle and attendant distraction of wine tasting or shopping or night life. It's the day when nearly everyone takes a breather and, indeed, we found we had the whole town of Calistoga pretty much to ourselves.

We were the only guests at the Inn. The management kindly left us a key tucked away in a secret place. We walked the nearly deserted main street and enjoyed a quiet so complete we could hear the far off call of a hawk. We took in the spectacular views past the steaming hot springs resorts up to the flanks of Mount St. Helena and the looming cliffs of the Palisades.

The Calistoga Inn has a small wooden balcony overlooking Lincoln Avenue, the main street. The balcony holds a little table and two chairs, perhaps the best dining seats in the whole town. We laid out a simple meal of paté and cheese with bread, strong mustard and cornichons. With the uncommonly sparse parade on the street, we spent the afternoon relishing our food, good red wine, and the comings and goings of the few window shoppers, some kids on brand new bicycles, and a few elderly locals out strolling in the brittle winter sunshine.

Yountville Festival of Lights
944-0904
See November.

Carols in the Caves
224-4222
See November.

Pioneer Christmas
Bale Grist Mill State Historic Park
963-2236
Nineteenth-century Napa Valley reenacted.

9
Napa Valley
On Location

The Napa Valley has long been a favorite of Hollywood for movie shoots, going back to at least 1940. Disney's 1960 classic **Pollyanna** is the most famous film shot in the Valley, but another Disney film shot locally, **The Parent Trap**, is an equally enjoyable film.

Commercials by the score, several TV movies, and even TV series also have the Valley stamp. The most famous TV series was **Falcon Crest**, shot on location west of St. Helena on Spring Mountain. During that show's heyday in the late '80s and early '90s, many St. Helena locals had the experience of having a neighborhood walk interrupted by being hailed from the rolled-down window of a car, "Is this the way to Falcon Crest?"

"No Ma'am, you're on Spring Street, you want Spring Mountain Road, other side of town."

Those questions have mostly stopped now that Spring Mountain Winery no longer offers tours. Still, it's easy to imagine that requests for filming in the Napa Valley will only increase in the future.

In this chapter we provide a synopsis and review of all the on-location films we could find from the local video store and library system. Two films, **The Bees** and **This Earth Is Mine**, we could not find copies to review, but list anyway along with comments by other reviewers. It's not an exhaustive list, and you might have fun tracking down films we've missed. By the way, some of the filming locations would be a fun site for a picnic.

Ratings System

1 wine bottle: vinegar-forming bacteria spoiled the wine

2 wine bottles: some interesting elements but didn't quite reach balance

3 wine bottles: a decent table wine

4 wine bottles: elements of greatness—maybe the next vintage

5 wine bottles: bottled poetry

■ Films Shot in the Napa Valley

A Walk in the Clouds
Directed by Alfonso Arau
1995

If you're partial to romantic dramas and know nothing about the wine industry, this film might pass muster, but many unauthentic and inaccurate scenes are so ludicrous that grape growers and wine makers will be laughing out loud.

World War II has just ended as Paul Sutton (Keanu Reeves) returns to San Francisco, his wife whom he barely knows, and his job as a chocolate salesman. Haunted by memories of the battles, Sutton is a changed man and wants a far different life than his wife does. On a derailed business trip to Sacramento, he meets Victoria Aragon (Altara Sanchez-Gijon), a graduate student whose traditional Mexican father will be horrified and dishonored when he learns she is pregnant out of wedlock. In an act of bold chivalry, Sutton volunteers to be her 'husband' to soften the blow. Victoria's father (Giancarlo Giannini) is hostile and suspicious of the new husband, but the patriarch of the family (Anthony Quinn) bestows his blessing and will play a key role as cupid to keep the couple together.

The first in a series of technical blunders by the filmmakers occurs on the first night. Though it's still late summer, we're asked to believe a potentially killing frost strikes a day before the harvest. With Victoria in a thin nightgown and Sutton in a T-shirt (remember it's below freezing), we witness a ballet with strap-on butterfly wings as they successfully keep the heat from the orchard heaters near the ground with just the right choreography. The next day is harvest (typically frost season and harvest are separated by at least four months) and a foot-stomping grape crush in a giant redwood vat ensues though more efficient (and sanitary) techniques for crushing had been used here since the 19th century.

An honorable but sad Sutton returns to his wife in San Francisco only to find an annulment form that sets him free. He formally asks for the hand of the Aragon daughter but Giannini is angry, and in the fight that follows, a lantern sets the entire vineyard aflame without touching the drier surrounding brush and forest. All is lost until Sutton remembers the mother vine Quinn has brought from Spain from which the vineyard has been propagated. With the strength hitherto required of a D2 Caterpillar tractor, Reeves yanks the vine out of the dry ground roots and all. The roots are alive and the vineyard is replanted to all its former splendor.

A touching ending but for one problem: Rootstock is not taken from the roots but from branch cuttings. By pulling the vine clear of the ground and killing it Sutton actually destroyed whatever chance they had to replant. Well, whatever. Lots of pretty scenes shot at Mount Veeder Winery, Beringer Vineyards, Charles Krug, and Duckhorn Vineyards.

Black Rain
Directed by Ridley Scott
1989

In this film-noir cop-chaser, master filmmaker Ridley Scott does for the streets of Tokyo what he did for Los Angeles in his masterpiece **Blade Runner**. Nick Conklin (Michael Douglas) is a tough, slightly crooked New York cop styled after Clint Eastwood's Dirty Harry character. The opening scene shows us that Douglas is just a little bit crazy too, in a motorcycle race along an obstacle-strewn New York waterfront. He and his partner Charlie (Andy Garcia) are drawn into the Japanese mafia underworld when they witness a daring daylight murder in a restaurant.

His adversary, Sato, is Douglas's mirror image, a rogue in the Japanese crime world, a good-guy/bad-guy match-up exemplified in Akira Kurosawa's **Runaway Train**. After Sato's capture, Douglas reluctantly escorts the extradited criminal to Japan but makes a stupid error in signing away his captive to the wrong people on an insurance form he can't read. This blunder sets the stage for an intense manhunt in which Douglas has few allies but an expatriate call girl from Chicago (Kate Capshaw) and Japanese police inspector Masahiro (Ken Takakura), a 'suit' for whom Douglas at first has nothing but contempt. There's a great bar scene that allows a break in the intensity when comedian Garcia encourages the reluctant and embarrassed Takakura to sing Ray Charles for the audience. When Garcia is ambushed and killed by Sato's motorcycle gang, a tentative partnership starts to form between Douglas and Takakura.

A second power struggle between underworld rivals Sato and Sugai leads to shootouts in a steel factory and finally to a grapevine-trellised countryside retreat, actually filmed on the Domain Chandon property on Mount Veeder. A high-speed motorcycle chase along steep hillside terraces brings the film full circle. The Japanese pagoda built on a hilltop for the movie is still there if you have a chance to tour the property.

This is a highly entertaining, coherent film, with great acting by Douglas, eerie lighting effects á la Scott, and some surprises that will keep you riveted.

The Bees
Directed by Alfredo Zacharias
1978

Grade B horror/thriller flick stars John Carradine, John Saxon and Angel Tompkins, South American killer bees are smuggled into the United States where a team of scientists tries to stop them. They soon mutate into a super-intelligent race and threaten the entire world. Some comments from Internet Movie Data Base (IMBD): "This must be the funniest bad film of modern times . . . A seventies counterpart of Ed Wood's earlier classics." Video Hound's Golden Movie Retriever calls it a "cheap ripoff of The Swarm, which is saying something." Filming locations include Yountville, St. Helena and Calistoga. As for rating, we haven't seen it yet but Video Hound gives it big bad WOOF!

Dying Young
Directed by Joel Schumacher
1991

Julia Roberts stars as Hillary O'Neill, a tough young beauty from Oakland who dumps her cheating boyfriend in the first scenes. Going against her unsympathetic mother's advice to take him back, she lands a job as caregiver for a rich but terminally ill leukemia patient Victor Gettings (Campbell Scott), despite a total lack of nursing skills. Roberts' leonine head of red hair and leggy good looks are the real-life flip side of the models painted by the German Impressionists Scott is studying for his Ph.D. thesis. Literally sick of the chemotherapy treatment and wanting desperately to believe love will heal, he forsakes his father's and doctor's advice and takes a romantic cottage on the coast, filmed in the town of Mendocino. The all-too-brief interlude of romance ends when Scott once again falls sick.

The film desperately wants to be a tear-jerker but with the overworked theme of young love tragically cut short and the lack of standout performances by the cast, it falls short of its goal. Some scenes are shot in the upper Napa Valley when the couple visit the winery of a friend.

Gates of Heaven
Directed by Errol Morris
1978

This film documents a portion of the pet cemetery business in northern California by interviewing the principal players. At first unsure whether the film's tone is tongue-in-cheek, we slowly come to appreciate the people and the philosophy they embrace. The first half documents the demise of a pet cemetery in Los Altos, the second half a success story in the hills outside Napa. At the crux of the issue is the question, "Do our pets go to heaven?" Mainstream Christianity says no. Calvin Harberts, founder and owner of Bubbling Well Pet Cemetery, believes an all-compassionate God is concerned with all living things, not just those on two legs. The success of the business shows many agree.

This is an interesting look at an unusual industry. It includes revealing panoramic shots of an untouched Atlas Peak Road before development.

Howard the Duck
Directed by Willard Huyck
1986

An unusual bomb from George Lucas, shot out of the water by critics and movie goers. Howard is accidentally sucked into a laser vortex and transported from Duck World to Earth, where he befriends rock musician Lea Thompson ('Caroline in the City') and saves the planet from hideous Dark

Overlords. The alien duck concept starts promising but gets lost in corny dialogue and lame chase scenes. Children may like the simple plot and special effects. Jeffrey Jones' transformation from scientist to Dark Overlord host body is fun to watch. Tim Robbins plays the nerdy assistant.

Local scenes are a restaurant south of Napa (now gone) and an ultralight-flying sequence somewhere in the Delta.

Jack
Directed by Francis Ford Coppola
1996

Robin Williams is perfectly cast as a boy who grows at four times the normal human rate. By the time we see him at ten, he looks like a 40-year-old man with a ten-year-old's emotional development, come to think of it, not a great stretch for Williams. Despite an overprotective mother, he makes the transition from home schooling to public school with the help of his tutor (Bill Cosby), his teacher (a pre-sex-bomb Jennifer Lopez), and his best friend's vampy mom (Fran Drescher). Though the underlying theme is farfetched, the parallels it draws to ostracized kids and peer intolerance are close to the bone. A touching film. If you like Williams, you'll like this.

The façade of St. Helena Elementary School on Adams Street will be recognizable to all residents. Many students in town remember Williams' generous hospitality when filming here.

Moonraker
Directed by Lewis Gilbert
1979

James Bond (Roger Moore) must stop the evil but imperturbable Dr. Drax before he poisons the human race and replaces it with the perfect Aryantype super race. His mission takes him on location to Venice, Rio, the Amazon and outer space. Lots of high-speed chases and high-tech gizmos lead to the usual denouement and Q's immortal line, "I believe they're attempting re-entry, sir." The opening parachuting sequence is shot over Napa County with a clearly recognizable Lake Berryessa below.

No Rating (you know what to expect.)

Mumford
Directed by Lawrence Kasdan
1999

A new psychiatrist shows up in town and suddenly the other two practicing professionals are wondering where their business went. The youthful, good-looking shrink (Mumford, played by Loren Dean), whose career is skyrocketing, has a shady past. In addition, he starts to fall in love with a patient just before his past is revealed. Is there something in the wine here? It's a twist on the theme of **Wild in the Country**. Despite practicing psychiatry without a license, his innate empathy enables him to help everyone who seeks his advice. Understated direction by Kasdan sets the tone for believable if unspectacular performances by the cast. With Ted Danson, Martin Short, Robert Stack, and Jason Lee as Mumford's friend Skip, the skateboarding computer millionaire with his own secret.

There's a brief shot of downtown St. Helena and the Goodman's building.

Pollyanna
Directed by David Swift
1960

Hayley Mills as Polly Whittier is perfectly cast as a young orphan who transforms the sour old town of Harrington with her ability to always see the silver lining. The opening scene shows Kevin Corcoran as the boy orphan Jimmy Bean rolling a hoop in front of the Old Bale Mill. Much of this classic film is shot in the Valley, including the old St. Helena train depot. With Jane Wyman, Richard Egan, Adolphe Menjou, Agnes Moorehead as the cantankerous hypochondriac, and Karl Malden as The Reverend, who delivers a thunderous fire-and-brimstone sermon.

The Parent Trap
Directed by Nancy Meyers
1998

Unusual though it may be for the Wine Country film reviewer to gush over Disney films, this one's kind of special. It's a remake of course of the popular original starring Hayley Mills—didn't we all fall in love with her then? The storybook cruise-ship wedding of Nicolas Parker (Dennis Quaid) and Elizabeth James (Natasha Richardson) quickly ends in divorce with the families split between London and Napa Valley. The twin sisters (played by Lindsay Lohan) meet at an east coast summer camp and instantly become enemies until they discover the secret kept by their parents for twelve years. For that withheld knowledge, the otherwise doting parents deserve the trick played on them when sisters Annie and Hallie switch places and conspire to bring Quaid and Richardson back together. A major obstacle must be overcome when gold-digger publicist Meredith Blake has Quaid fast-tracking to the marriage chapel. The girls team up to get Blake out of the picture by playing some pretty mean pranks on a camping trip. True to a storybook tale, all ends happily ever after.

Perhaps the most common dream of every child of divorced parents, this movie is more relevant today than it was forty years ago. This is a delightful film with laughter and, yes, a tear or two, that will touch many hearts. Filmed partly on location at Staglin Family Vineyards.

They Knew What They Wanted
Directed by Garson Kanin
1940

An unlettered Italian immigrant to the Napa Valley formally woos a poor but attractive San Francisco waitress to be his wife. The characters are drawn simply with Charles Laughton as the good-hearted vineyard owner, Carole Lombard as his wife-to-be and William Gargan as Laughton's foreman who seduces Lombard. The day before the wedding Lombard confesses she is pregnant. Instead of ruining three lives, Laughton graciously forgives her.

The issue of a pregnant unmarried woman was daring in 1940, but modern audiences will yawn. Though well received at the time (Gargan received an Academy Award nomination for best supporting actor), the movie suffers from dated acting methods. The opening scene shows the upper Napa Valley with Mount St. Helena in the background and another with the Rutherford train station, signed "South Napa").

This Earth Is Mine
Directed by Henry King
1959

Elizabeth Rambeau (Jean Simmons) comes from England to live in California with her aunt and uncle, still wealthy despite the Depression. She hopes to marry a rich landowner, but runs into opposition from her cousin, John Rambeau (Rock Hudson). A struggle develops between John and Phillippe Rambeau (Claude Rains) over whether the family will sell to bootleggers. Comments from Internet Movie Database summarize this film: ". . . The acting and dialogue are stiff, and the story unfolds with all the gusto of watching wine ferment. If this was champagne, it would have been born flat." They reportedly used filming locations at many wineries up and down the Valley, including Beaulieu, Beringer, Charles Krug, Christian Brothers, Inglenook, Louis Martini, Mayacamas and Schramsberg.

Wild in the Country
Directed by Philip Dunne
1962

Elvis 'bad boy' Presley in a surprisingly serious role about a troubled but artistic youth at a crossroads. Elvis has girls aplenty and can't decide on which one until he falls for his beautiful parole psychiatrist (Hope Lange). When her feelings show against her better professional judgment, her reputation is nearly ruined. An early scene in which Elvis escapes by crossing a stream is shot at Casa Nuestra Winery. The most recognizable local landmark is the Ink House. A strong performance by Lange with Tuesday Weld as the 'bad girl.' Among the many mediocre films he did, this is one of the best Elvis films.

10
Heading In /Heading Out

On your way to and from the Napa Valley, you may want to take a little time to investigate the pleasures to be found in our neighboring counties. A list of helpful phone numbers and web addresses follows.

■ San Francisco and the Bay Area

A visit to the Napa Wine Country can begin or end with a stop in the dynamic San Francisco Bay Area. It's normally about an hour's drive between San Francisco/Oakland/Berkeley and Napa. A good way to start any Bay Area tour is with a copy of the **San Francisco Chronicle** or a visit to their web site at **www.sfgate.com.**

You might also want to contact the following helpful offices:

San Francisco Visitor's Center
415-391-2000
www.sfvisitor.org

Oakland Convention Center
510-839-9000
www.oaklandcvb.com
www.oaklandnet.com

Berkeley Chamber of Commerce
510-549-7000
www.berkeleychamber.com

Menlo Park Chamber of Commerce
650-325-2818
www.menloparkchamber.com

■ Sonoma County

Sonoma County lies just west of the Napa Valley and can easily be reached from Calistoga in the north via Highway 128, which winds scenically into the famed Alexander Valley wine-grape growing region.

Petrified Forest Road heads west from Highway 128 just north of Calistoga. This lovely winding road connects to Porter Creek Road and then to Mark West Springs Road, leading you to the north/south Highway 101 corridor between Santa Rosa and Healdsburg.

Mid-Valley, the very winding Oakville Grade heads east through the Sonoma-Napa hills to Trinity Road and the town of Glen Ellen in the Valley of the Moon.

Highway 12/121 passes through the Los Carneros growing region just south of Napa. This road splits at Schellville, where you can head north on Highway 12 to Sonoma and the Valley of the Moon, or continue west on Highway 121 to Petaluma. Please contact the following offices and addresses for more information:

**California Welcome Center and
Sonoma County Winery Association**
586-3795
www.sonomawine.com

**www.sonomapicnic.com—The Wine Country
Online.**

■ A Lovely Drive and a Visit to the Jimtown Store in the Alexander Valley

Open seven days a week until 5 p.m., the Jimtown Store is a great picnic food stop if you're coming or going to the Napa Valley from US 101 and the Healdsburg/Geyserville area of Sonoma County. This classic rural general store was founded in 1874 and has been in operation at the current location since 1893. With new owners in 1990, the old store in the heart of Sonoma County's beautiful Alexander Valley has become famous for good food and real coffee. An eccentric mix of merchandise and antiques is reminiscent of the days when major California highways were still tranquil two-lane blacktops winding through the countryside.

Follow State Highway 128 north out of Calistoga for about 17 miles. You'll pass through some exceptional ranchlands set in the rolling oak savanna on either side of the lovely Knights Valley, which is midway between Jimtown in the Alexander Valley and Calistoga in the Napa Valley.

The Jimtown Store
6708 State Hwy 128
Healdsburg 95448
433-1212
www.jimtown.com

■ Marin County

Situated just north of the Golden Gate and south of Sonoma County's Wine Country, Marin County is famous for its dramatic windblown coastal headlands and the inviting pastoral dairylands surrounding Tomales Bay.

Marin County Convention and Visitor's Bureau
415-472-7470
www.visitmarin.org

Point Reyes National Seashore
415-464-5100
www.nps.gov/pore

Golden Gate National Recreation Area
415-331-1540
www.nps.gov/goga

Tomales Bay Foods and The Cowgirl Creamery
415-663-9335
www.cowgirlcreamery.com

Hog Island Oyster Company
415-663-9218
www.hogislandoyster.com

■ Lake County

If you plan to come or go by way of Lake County, Highway 29 north from Calistoga skirts majestic Mount St. Helena, connecting to the Middletown and the Clear Lake areas.

Greater Lakeport Chamber of Commerce
263-5092
www.lakeportchamber.com

■ Yolo County and Points East

Highway 128 heads east out of Rutherford and winds its way past Lake Berryessa and down to the town of Winters and the Sacramento Valley.

Winters Chamber of Commerce
530-795-2329
www.winterschamber.com

Sacramento Chamber of Commerce
916-552-6800
www.metrochamber.org/

APPENDIX A
Getting Here/Mode of Travel

PUBLIC TRANSPORTATION

Greyhound Bus Lines
643-7661

Greyhound runs two busses a day between Vallejo and Napa. You can leave Vallejo at 12:30 p.m. or 5:30 p.m., arriving in Napa 35 to 40 minutes later. Busses leave Napa at 11:20 a.m. or 5:35 p.m. to return to Vallejo, where connections can be made to the San Francisco Bay Area or the Sacramento Valley. The Napa depot connects to local bus service throughout the Napa Valley.

Napa County Transportation Planning Agency
'The Vine,' Napa County's bus service. For detailed information call 800-696-6443, or visit online at **www.napanews.com.**
The Vine provides convenient service throughout the Valley on Route #10:
Monday through Friday 5:20 a.m. to 9:05 p.m.
Saturday 6:00 a.m. to 8:10 p.m.
Sunday 8:15 a.m. to 6:00 p.m.
No service on major holidays.

Yountville Shuttle
Thanks to the sponsorship of numerous area businesses and organizations, the town of Yountville runs a unique free fixed-route bus shuttle serving major area destinations, including the Veterans Home of California. Buses run Wednesday through Sunday, 9:00 a.m. to noon and 1:00 p.m. to 4:00 p.m.

On Wednesdays between spring and early fall, buses also run from 5:00 p.m. to 8:00 p.m. to serve the Yountville Farmers Market in the Vintage 1870 parking lot next to Compadres Restaurant. This is a great way to enjoy the Market's free entertainment, put together a picnic and leave your automobile behind!

Please call the Town staff at 944-8851 for more information on this wonderful service or look at www.transitinfo.org/Yountville

TAXI SERVICE

Taxi Cabernet, 963-2620
Napa Valley Cab, 707-257-6444

APPENDIX B
Lodging & Camping

LODGING

Beazley House
1910 First Street
Napa 94559
257-1649

Villagio Inn and Spa
6481 Washington Street
Yountville 94599
800-351-1133
Yountville's newest and most opulent.

Auberge du Soleil
180 Rutherford Hill Rd
Rutherford 94573
963-1211

Rancho Caymus
1140 Rutherford Cross Rd
Rutherford 94573
800-845-1777

Ambrose Bierce House
1515 Main Street
St. Helena 94574
963-3003

Cinnamon Bear Bed and Breakfast
1407 Kearney Street
St. Helena 94574
963-4653

Ink House Bed and Breakfast
1575 St. Helena Highway
St. Helena 94574
963-3890
   Come stay where Elvis filmed **Wild in the Country** *in 1962.*

Rustridge Inn Bed and Breakfast
2910 Lower Chiles Valley Road
St. Helena 94574
965-9353

Wine Country Victorian and Cottage
400 Meadowood Lane
St. Helena 94574
963-0852

Hotel St. Helena
1309 Main Street
St. Helena 94574
888-478-4355, 963-4388

Harvest Inn
1 Main Street
St. Helena 94574
963-9463

The Harvest Inn is a master work in brick and stone by legendary masons Danny Scott and Robert Gastelum. The main building was completed in 1982. It's worth the price of a room to be able to enjoy the grand fireplace, all built of hand-cut paving stones salvaged from the streets of San Francisco.

Silver Rose Inn
351 Rosedale
Calistoga 94515
9429581

Triple S Ranch
4600 Mountain Home Ranch Road
Calistoga 94515
942-6730

CAMPING

Skyline Wilderness Park
2201 Imola Avenue
Napa 94558
252-0481

Bothe-Napa Valley State Park
3801 North St. Helena Highway
Calistoga 94515
942-4575

APPENDIX C
Resources

SUGGESTED READING

Allegra, Antonia, *Napa Valley: The Ultimate Winery Guide*, Chronicle Books, 1997.

Archuleta, Kay, *The Brannan Saga*, Calistoga, 1977.

Brewer, William H., *Up and Down California in 1860-1864*, Berkeley, UC Press, 1966.
The famous surveying crew visited Napa Valley in 1861.

Calkins, Victoria, *The Wappo People*, Pileated Press, 1994.

Conaway, James, *Napa*, Avon Books, 1992.
The controversial best seller.

Dutton, Joan Parry, *They Left Their Mark: Famous Passages through the Wine Country*, Illuminations Press, 1983.

Goss, Helen Rocca, *Life and Death of a Quicksilver Mine*, The Historical Society of Southern California, 1958.
Perhaps the classic of its kind, the author's father was superintendent of the Great Western Mine on Mount St. Helena for 30 years.

Issler, Anne Roller, *Our Mountain Hermitage: Silverado and Robert Louis Stevenson*, Stanford University Press, 1950.

Johnston, Moira, *Spectral Evidence: An American Family and the Recovered Memory Wars*, Houghton Mifflin, 1997.
The dark side of the American dream.

Lyon, Richards and Ruygt, Jake, *One Hundred County Roadside Wildflowers*, Stonecrest Press, 1996.

Pond, Janice E., *Stubbed Toes and Grapevines*, Napa River Press, 1996.
Charming vignettes of growing up in old-time Napa Valley.

Stanton, Ken, *Mount St. Helena and Robert Louis Stevenson State Park*, a *History and Guide*, Bonnie View Books, 1993.

Stanton, Ken, *Great Day Hikes in and around Napa Valley*, second edition, Bored Feet Press, 2001.

Stevenson, Robert Louis, *Silverado Squatters*, Lewis Osbourne, 1974.

Wright, Elizabeth Cyrus, *Early Upper Napa Valley*, Society of California Pioneers, 1949.

WEB GUIDE AND SUGGESTED BROWSING

www.napavalleyonline.com
  Complete guide to wine, food, lodging, spas, maps, etc.

Yogi Bear Home Page is found at:
www.aristotle.net/~cgsports
  History, photos and a recording of the Yogi Bear theme song!

California State Home Page: www.ca.gov

How Far is it?: www.indo.com/distance

KPIX TV Channel 5, San Francisco:
www.kpix.com

Marin, Sonoma and Napa County Music Events:
www.northbaymusic.com

GUIDE TO LOCAL NEWSPAPERS

Napa Valley Register
1615 Second Street
Napa 94559
226-3711
Napa's only daily.

Napa County Record
1320 Second Street
Napa 94559
252-8877

Napa Sentinel
1627 Lincoln Avenue
Napa 94559
257-6272

St. Helena Star
1328 Main Street
St. Helena 94574
963-2731
Napa Valley's oldest paper, founded in 1874.

The Weekly Calistogan
1328 Main Street
St. Helena 94574
942-6242
Rolling the presses since 1877.

LOCAL RADIO STATIONS

KVYN AM 1440 ·
Voice of the North Bay since 1948. News/talk format.

KVYN FM 99.3
Adult contemporary music and news

KNDL FM 89.9
Voice of Pacific Union College in Angwin

KGRP FM 100.9
Light rock

SOME FAVORITE PICNIC WINES

Jeff Prather of Wine.com List:
97 Chappellet Chenin Blanc

99 Honig Sauvignon Blanc

96 Ballentine Vineyards Merlot Estate

99 Frog's Leap Leapfrogmilch

97 Adella Zinfandel

98 Luna Pinot Grigio

97 St. Supery Cabernet Sauvignon

Wines of Summer & two guys on wine
99 CosentinoTennero Rosso,

98 Cosentino Semillion

99 Elyse Rose

99 Elyse Dlíaventure

■ Acknowledgments

We would like to thank the many people without whom this book would not have been possible. They expressed interest and encouraged us, took time out of their busy days for special tours, and sent us valuable information.

In no particular order we extend our gratitude to Jim O'Shay, Olga Korbeck, Ray Particelli, John Lahey, Bob Childs, Sandee Betterton, Andy Pestoni, Roger Asbill, J. Paul Dumont, Laurie Gepford, Nat Komes, Toni Nichelini-Irwin, Kevin Corley, Linda McGee, Yvonne Gray, Tanya Mufich, Bruce Willis, Annie Margadant, Robert Kresko, Jane Fairley, Sally Wood, Jim and Imogene Prager, Charles Neate, Bill Grummer, Shay Boswell, Richard Graeser, Vickie Gott, Reece Baswell, Liza Russ, Kevin Karl, and Judy Ann Pridmore. Antone Fahden gave us a wonderful tour of his gardens. Mick Winter shared key information for the movie chapter. Napa Valley Vintners provided the source map for our appellation map. The Napa, St. Helena and Calistoga Chambers of Commerce were rich sources of material. Last but not least, thanks to William Heintz for his meticulous research on Wine Country history, which allowed us to get a grasp on the subject.

KS

I would especially like to acknowledge the courtesy and good Napa County spirit and hospitality with which I was treated during my research for this book.

It was not without some trepidation that, I, a native of far off Detroit, Michigan and now a long time Sonoma County resident, undertook the task of writing a book about "rival" Napa County.

It was great good fortune that I was able to team up with Ken Stanton, a long term Napa County resident, grape grower, and distinguished local author.

My thanks to Ken, and heartfelt thank yous to all the folks mentioned above, and others too numerous to mention who took the time to contribute to my continuing education into the ways of Napa County's remarkable community.

JB

■ Photograph and Illustration Credits

Page	Photograph/Illustration	Credit
Front	Cover	Kaarin Svendsen
Back	Cover Cartoon	Elizabeth Leeds
2	Trail above vineyards	Kaarin Svendsen
10	White Sulphur Creek	Jack Burton
13	Black Obsidian arrow point	Janette Burton
14	Wappo basket	Janette Burton
15	Stone Barn in Knights Valley	Ken Stanton
16	Vineyard in the mist	Jack Burton
18	Old carriage wagon, Pope Valley	Ken Stanton
22	"No picnicking"	Ken Stanton
23	Old dry stackwork	Jack Burton
25	Bennet Bridge, Calistoga	Ken Stanton
36	Two goats	Bodega Goat Cheese
42	Swartz Creek Bridge	Ken Stanton
46	Old Soda Canyon Bridge	Jack Burton
47	Sycamores nr Oakville Cross Rd	Ken Stanton
48	Napa Valley olives	Jack Burton
51	Bridge near Palisades	Ken Stanton
55	Stonework at Rudd Vineyards	Ken Stanton
70	Bridge on Old Sonoma Road	Ken Stanton
71	Regusci Winery	Ken Stanton
73	Grapes at harvest	Liz Petersen
76	Bridge at Zinfandel Lane	Ken Stanton
80	Cabernet harvest	Ken Stanton
82	Springtime along the Silverado Trail	Jack Burton
84	Graeser Winery	Ken Stanton
85	Hans Fahden Winery	Ken Stanton
86	Old building at Nichelini	Ken Stanton
87	Pope Valley Winery	Ken Stanton
89	Waterwheel at Bale Grist Mill	Jack Burton
91	Cabernet grapes	Liz Petersen
92	Pope Street Bridge	Ken Stanton
94	Historic Garnett Creek Bridge	Ken Stanton
96	Oak Shores Picnic Area	Ken Stanton
103	Trancas Bridge	Ken Stanton
109	Greystone, St. Helena	Jack Burton
115	Olive grove at St. Clement	Jack Burton
117	Modern Southern Crossing Bridge	Ken Stanton
118	Old wall in Knights Valley	Ken Stanton
123	Old church at Calistoga	Jack Burton
129	Old tractor at special event	Ken Stanton
130	Bridge at Highway 128	Ken Stanton
133	Seminary Street Bridge, Napa	Ken Stanton
135	Old stones at Bale Mill	Jack Burton
149	Film clapper board	Wendy Blakeway

■ Index

■ About Bored Feet

We began Bored Feet Press in 1986 to publish *The Hiker's hip pocket Guide to the Mendocino Coast*. We've grown our company by presenting the most accurate guidebooks for California, including our series on California's Coastal Trail.

Updates on our publications are now available on our website, **boredfeet.com**, where you can also easily provide your feedback on any of our books, or order any of our products. If you'd rather have a catalog, please send or call in your name and address. The list below represents only 20 % of our books, with many of our bestsellers. We also have hiking and recreation maps to many areas of the west.

Napa Valley Picnic/Burton&Stanton	$15.00
Sonoma Picnic/ Burton	13.00
Great Day Hikes . . . Napa Valley, 2nd ed./ Stanton	15.00
Hiking the California Coastal Trail, Vol.1:	
Oregon-Monterey, 2nd ed.	19.50
Hiking the California Coastal Trail, Vol. 2:	
Monterey-Mexico	19.00
Hiking the California Coastal Trail, Complete Set	37.00
Trails & Tales of Yosemite & the Central Sierra	16.00
Hiker's hip pocket Guide to Sonoma County, 2nd ed.	15.00
Hiker's hip pocket Guide to Humboldt Coast, 2nd ed.	14.00
Hiker's hip pocket Guide to Mendocino Coast, 3rd ed.	14.00
Hiker's hip pocket Guide to Mendocino Highlands	16.00
Mendocino Coast Bike Rides/Lorentzen	16.00
Geologic Trips: San Francisco & Bay Area/Konigsmark	13.95
A Tour of Mendocino: 32 Historic Buildings / Bear	7.00
Wood, Water, Air & Fire: Anthology of Mendocino Women Poets	19.00

Please add $3 shipping for orders under $30, $6 over $30 ($5 / 8 for rush)
For shipping to a California address, please add 7.25 % tax.
PRICES SUBJECT TO CHANGE WITHOUT NOTICE.

BORED FEET PRESS
P.O.Box 1832
Mendocino, CA 95460
888-336-6199
707-964-6629
FAX 707-964-5953
www.boredfeet.com